Poetry Ireland Review 122

Eagarthóir / Editor
EAVAN BOLAND

Poetry Ireland Ltd / Éigse Éireann Teo gratefully acknowledges the assistance of The Arts Council / An Chomhairle Ealaíon and The Arts Council of Northern Ireland.

Poetry Ireland invites individuals and commercial organizations to become Friends of Poetry Ireland. For more details, please contact:

Poetry Ireland Friends Scheme, Poetry Ireland, 11 Parnell Square East, Dublin 1, Ireland

or telephone +353 1 6789815; e-mail info@poetryireland.ie

FRIENDS:
Joan and Joe McBreen, Desmond Windle, Neville Keery, Noel and Anne Monahan, Ruth Webster, Maurice Earls, Mary Shine Thompson, Seán Coyle, Henry and Deirdre Comerford, Thomas Dillon Redshaw, Rachel Joynt, Helen Flanagan

Poetry Ireland Review is published three times a year by Poetry Ireland Ltd. The Editor enjoys complete autonomy in the choice of material published. The contents of this publication should not be taken to reflect either the views or the policy of the publishers.

ISBN: 978-1-902121-65-9
ISSN: 0332-2998

ASSISTANT EDITOR: Paul Lenehan, with the assistance of Sarah Guinan, Matlyn Drucker, Megan Shaw, and Orla Higgins

IRISH-LANGUAGE EDITOR: Caitlín Nic Íomhair

DESIGN: Alistair Keady (www.hexhibit.com)

COVER CREDIT: from 'Dressed for Success' by Kelly Ratchford (www.kellyratchford.com)

Contents

POETRY IRELAND REVIEW 122

Editorial

THE CONSCRIPTED POET

In his 1974 volume called *Out of My Time*, John Hewitt included a memorable poem called 'The Scar'. It's just sixteen lines long and has the slight look of a sonnet that outgrew its living quarters. Nevertheless, short as it is, it records a powerful drama.

The poem's narrative notes the death of Hewitt's great-grandmother who went to the window during the 1847 famine intending to help a famine victim. Instead, she caught a fever from him and died. Hewitt summarizes the effect of this history on his own identity in two beautiful lines:

> ... that chance meeting, that brief confrontation,
> conscribed me of the Irishry for ever.

That word 'conscribed' – arcane and complicated though it may be – is compelling, both in and beyond the poem. It has caught my attention again while editing *Poetry Ireland Review*. The idea of the conscripted poet is always a controversial one, but never irrelevant. It remains central to the idea of a poet's role. But not always comfortably so, as a small, painful anecdote shows. It involves WH Auden, who went to the front in the Spanish Civil War. He then published a chapbook called *Spain* – really an extended poem just twelve pages long – in the key year of 1937. The last lines of the poem extend the Marxist conversation of that moment:

> History to the defeated
> May say Alas but cannot help or pardon.

Two years later Auden left Britain for the US. He went to say goodbye to his friend Stephen Spender. In Spender's account, Auden, catching sight of the chapbook on Spender's mantelpiece, went over and opened it to the last page. He then took out his pen, struck out the final lines and wrote in the margin: *This is a lie.*

This seems to me now both an act of honesty and a cautionary tale. It shows the fear a conscripted poet might have – conscripted that is by external forces – that their art might eventually be compromised in the cause of morality.

What the poet owes or doesn't owe to the world around him or her is a familiar subject. Conscription adds another layer: conscribing a poet to a cause, or an event, or an occasion, or an ideology, may sound coercive.

But the fact remains that many poets of worth and reach have been taken out of their comfort zone by an occasion or commitment and have documented that transit with powerful work. Yet today, so much has changed – so many new voices, so many different tonal registers – that the idea of the conscripted poet has had to change as well.

Today's conscripted poet still exists of course – and in the old version of the concept: poets of colour, environmentalist poets, political activists and others are still everywhere called to large questions and to make powerful, unsettling poems in the light of them. But in a new context, the poet we see today may also be conscribed differently: less by history or an external cause than by the subterranean conversation within poetry itself.

Patrick Kavanagh's comments on the Irish Revival – resisting it at every point – which I quote in a tribute in this issue, can be seen in this light as a form of counter-conscription. Alvy Carragher's bold persona poem – she is the featured poet in this issue – gestures towards a partly hidden poetic conversation, where definitions of the page and the performance vie with each other for clarification. Richard Murphy's rich and thoughtful interview in this issue describes the inward power of migration, geographical and imaginative. And there are many other poems in this issue where the poet is plainly and eloquently struggling to balance lyric poise with large ideas. It makes for exciting reading.

Does this mean that the idea of the conscripted poet is no longer of use? I don't think so. Looking at this issue of *PIR* is a reminder that the definition of the conscripted poet doesn't need to be abandoned, just broadened. In that sense the demands on the poet, the tensions within the poem, remain similar if not exactly the same. What is the same is the need for poetic rigour and thoughtfulness. No poet, after all, wants to accuse their words of falsehood in the margin of their own poem.

– **Eavan Boland**

Jennie Malboeuf

LANDSCAPE WHERE I MISS MY MOTHER

In it is the moon, for certain.
A rabbit distracting advancing foxes
from her young. A wren amusing me
in the same way. There would be a river
because there was one. A nearby haunted zoo
where every fall a horseman chased a small train
down a hill.
        I cannot think of my mother without
thinking of myself. This is the true test:
she made herself a shadow, tiny prey.
Somewhere in the line of the almost
too-distant, where the scene looks deep
but flat and fake, soft mountains behind
the sharp sublime, a house. Puffs of smoke
from the working chimney. A picnic table
crowded with nightshades and stonefruit.
A load of handsewn laundry hung out to dry
and forgotten.

Nessa O'Mahony

SUPER MOON ON THE M6

All dusk it was glare;
oncoming headlights flaring
over the median,
world tunnelling light
to the grey verge,
dented tin sides
of lorries slow-laning,
hemming me in
as I left the sun behind.

Then a disc so bright
it made me laugh out loud
when I finally recognised her,
my knuckles wheel-clenched,
after so many miles
of straight lines.

She was rising as I set
my way homeward,
floating like a parachute
in reverse,
arcing up over flatlands,
bogs, towns, silhouettes
unless cathode flared them.

The Shannon crossed,
outline of swans
like shades of the past
though I couldn't wait for them.

She might have filled the sky,
so pink her intention,
so inflated her will, so strong
her pull the road curved
away from her.

Graham Allen

WHERE IS THAT PARSEE TOWER OF SILENCE?

Death is contagious, the kingdom of worms.
It is an active element in the universe.
It is not subject to sanitation.
If you touch it you are lost, but Death touches everything.
It is the voice of a deranged hag screaming at the summer wind.
It is in the come to bed eyes of the hot politician.
It is a tic under the skin of each new born child.
No segregation tames it. No exposure to the sky.
Death marks the rise and fall of all faith, all ritual.
Our scientists have failed to master it.
Our teachers call it imageless and move on.
Only carrion befriend it, waiting eagerly for our cast-offs.
Our desolate astodans, built beyond the walls
that protect us from landslide, fire and flood,
are crammed with the dead and their time-bleached bones.
Such centres of gravity and tears, as they lower the feast
of Dignam down, are the eyes and ears of our fevered city.
Drowning they say is the pleasantest.

Roisin Kelly

SACRED HEART

I watch your spliff's ambered end trace the air
as it comes to your lips and leaves again.
Beyond the window, January's ash flakes away,

wet rooftops weeping grey light.
How did I get here from the island,
where once I watched the blink of Achill's lighthouse,

or from my mother's kitchen where a red bulb burns
before the Sacred Heart?
My dreams are of walking the beach at night

where the tide hisses to nothing and nothing.
For miles it leaves me babies along the shore, all thin
wet limbs and the eyes of aliens.

In the dark I know them by their failing hearts,
which beat as dim red lamps in each translucent body
and edge their beds of foam with fire.

Fred Johnston

CONFLICT

I want to write a poem of protest
but I'm aware I might upset someone
I might upset you –

this is the difficulty; how to protest softly
how to smack the metal without
putting a dent in it

how not to become an enemy of the state
of poetry, which has spies everywhere –

how to infiltrate, remain invisible
to pass through checkpoints and not
have my words confiscated

to have no part of me put at risk
yet to make a sound, a mousy squeak
perhaps, but a sound nonetheless –

a sound I can call my own
yet a note that rings out somewhere

under the rubble, in the drains,
in the bombed air
or does nothing else but simply be –

that's sufficient, to be word enough
in landscapes of silence

to put that word in a single mouth
a miracle in itself,
a rage in a small thing. But can I do this

and stay harmless, out of the watch
of prizes, honours, my own ambition?
Can I hurl my words and run away?

Julie Morrissy

CIVIL REGULATIONS AMENDMENT ACT 1956: RETIREMENT OF WOMEN CIVIL SERVANTS ON MARRIAGE

10 (1) Women holding positions in the civil service other than positions which are declared excepted positions under subsection 2 of this section are required to retire upon marriage.

--(2) The minister may from time to time declare any particular positions (not being established positions) or class of positions to be excepted positions for the purpose of subsection 1 of this section.

hold women / position women / service women / other women / declare women / except

women / require women / establish women / retire women / purpose women / section women

the minister holds women in sub positions

positions women in marriage

the minister others women, declares women for service

the minister excepts women from being civil

retires women for other purposes

the minister purposes women to marriage

establishes service positions for women

women from women of women upon women for women to women in

women hold / women position / women declare / women require / women establish

May women declare positions other than service?

May women declare positions other than marriage?

May women be excepted from being civil?

Minister, may we?

Seán Hewitt

AT THE EDGE OF THESE THINGS

Rachael Boast, *Void Studies* (Picador Poetry, 2016), £9.99.
Tom French, *The Way to Work* (The Gallery Press, 2016), €12.50.
Jacob Polley, *Jackself* (Picador Poetry, 2016), £9.99.

Rachael Boast's poetry has long explored the philosophical reach of the lyric, unweaving difficult ideas into a music of graceful simplicity. Her new work, *Void Studies*, testifies to a deep intelligence, realising a proposed project of the French Symbolist poet Arthur Rimbaud, in which he hoped to write a series of poems as musical *études*, calling up the spirit of their subject through patterns of rhythm and assonance. Though this sounds like an academic project, verging on the esoteric, Boast's skill in these mostly ten-line poems is to elucidate the slipperiness of the tone poem through the very slipperiness of her ideas, so that the poems are, in some way, a token of the speaker's need 'to be ever at the edge of these things'. It is hard to describe the movement of thought within these *études*, with each idea giving way to a new one that seems to sit just on the brink of consciousness. In 'Album', Boast gives the best description of this process as 'thought latching onto thought and pulling'.

Although these poems do create strong musical atmospheres, they are far from being what the blurb describes as 'pure music': in fact, they are full of quiet observation, scenes in which the smallest movement is noted and explored. Above all, they seem to be meditations on love and its formal requirements, 'how love cannot / entirely belong to us not because / it wants to but because it must'. Love, as something in many ways being constantly negotiated in these poems, finds its mirror in the careful and elusive movements of the verse itself. 'Special Reserve', one of the finest poems in the collection, demonstrates the ways in which Boast can tack between the lightly-held emotion and the carefully traced thought:

> When you leave you never quite leave,
> keeping me at the edge of your vision
> as the days fill with other people
> whose voices now and then rise
> above the radio you seldom switch off
> for how it drowns in sonatas
> the events of a day and cleanses them,
> even when asleep, or when, if ever,
> you think back to what happened
> before what happened before

and find me again, with not much to say,
sitting on the bank of the river with you
speaking in soft voices of the commonplace,
for the heart must surely speak that way.

The scope of the sonnet, the movement towards those last two lines, is measured by a poet unafraid to qualify or correct her thought as she travels; speaking 'in soft voices', yes, but guiding the reader unfailingly through.

Tom French, similarly, speaks with a 'soft voice', drawing on a familiar Irish pastoral which, as with the poetry of Longley and Heaney, is imbued with the political. His latest collection, *The Way to Work*, is relatively long (just under 100 pages), and is rooted in local detail, local characters. Some, like 'Nana' and 'East', are full of family references, and clearly have an emotional core, but sometimes this fails to implicate the reader. Likewise, some of the smaller poems in this collection are beautifully formed, both in their sentiment and their composition, whereas others seem one step short of completion. French has a knack for understatement, as the two-line poem 'A Gift' shows perfectly:

We gave away more than a garden fork and *sleán*
when we gave away his garden fork and *sleán*.

In the best of these lyrics, French moves carefully towards the core of the poem, taking from the initial subject a series of deft turns of thought. In 'Heron', the bird of the title features only in the very first line, as a springboard towards something more surprising and unexpected:

It is the spit of Rabbi Hillel,
forced by some toe-rag to recite,
on one foot, at sword point,
the whole Torah from memory,

who condensed it, as it must
ever after be condensed –
'Love neighbour. Love God.
The rest is commentary.'

The same powerful understatement is carried through in a number of other short poems, such as 'The Sixth of March' and 'Pig Sty, Janeville'. In others, like 'The Butter Box, Janeville', neither the image nor the idea seems strong enough to carry the poem home. There is, on occasion, a too heavy reliance on the reader to infer something profound from an image or recalled conversation. 'Asking Dennis O'Driscoll in What Was

Waterstone's about Ted Lean's Hair', a poem whose title does the majority of scene-setting, but which takes six lines to set the scene nonetheless, ends on an observation that seems to suggest it carries more weight than it does:

> he says he can see
> Ted Lean's white mane
> clearly to this day
>
> because Ted Lean had the same
> white mane Ted's father had.

It feels, in a number of these poems, as though the concluding thought is missing; as if the poet is behind the scenes suggesting that he knows more than we do. We are not always quite certain, however, whether he does or not. Overall, *The Way to Work* is a quiet but formally-astute book, though there are weaker poems which, on reflection, do not quite earn their keep in what is a longer than average collection.

Whereas French and Boast write in 'the soft voices of the commonplace', Jacob Polley's TS Eliot prize-winning new work, *Jackself,* set in the fictional village of Lamanby, is full of nursery-rhyme rhythms and the unsettling darkness of English folklore, counterpointing sardonic humour with passages of deep tenderness. Polley's language wears its energy outwardly, with its narrative fusing the lyrical with the violent in a startling and often funny way: 'see, Wren says, clapping Jackself on the back / as he retches that's a proper poem for you / agony to bring up, / with real carrots in it'. Beginning with a cinematic scan over a northern landscape, Polley draws us into the village, 'home of shadows heart of the wind', before we meet Jackself. A wry, creeping character, Jackself is a loner: he has an air of threat, he is disaffected, he eats alone in a coal-shed. That is before he meets Jeremy Wren, himself a sarcastic, abused, sombre character, who becomes a drinking partner and friend.

In fact, where this book begins as a sort of gothic narrative, both disturbing and inventive, it becomes a study of friendship and the stark loss of innocence, at times quite terrifying in its effect. Although we sense the menace of the book from the beginning (after we are introduced to Jackself, there is a double page spread with the words 'DON'T WAKE HIM' in large bold type), Polley skilfully uncovers the emotional heart of his narrative in the poem 'Jack Frost'. Jackself, in his 'Jack Frost' incarnation, is covering up the cars and shrubs with ice, before stopping to rest 'among the gallows-poles of the moonlit playground'. Here, he sees Wren walking despondently down the road 'wearing snow-globe deely boppers, a mantle of tinsel':

you look a proper sight, Jackself says
Wren's weeping the lucid mask that's welding to his cheekbones
help me, he says, keep everything just as it is

And so a dark, wry series of poems about the moody teenage Jackself begins to turn. Polley masterfully reveals and draws out a heart-wrenching tale of mental illness, suicide, and its aftermath. Thoroughly readable, complex and deeply-felt, Jackself demonstrates the power of narrative poetry, and has proved itself to be one of the most original and compelling books of recent years.

Mary Woodward

THE MINER

was here a week, while they were fund-raising in the town.
I tidied up the kitchen cupboard to make space; he put in

a bag of sugar, a jar of raspberry jam and a packet of tea.
He chain-smoked, maybe once or twice stayed and watched

the news with me. He was quiet, reserved, cautiously polite.
Then he moved on somewhere else. After the strike I heard

he'd started driving a van. All that time I knew I owed him,
as everyone did, awkwardly, without knowing how to say it.

What was a yard of shelf, a rent free room? I didn't talk
about Matthew McDonagh, who'd leave Cuilmore and Sligo

each year to work in some nameless South Wales pit,
who, one summer, did not arrive back home, never saw

his little girls again, nor met the new baby, my grandmother;
whose memories of light green hills and cold silver streams

burned and suffocated in a blinding thunderstorm of coal,
who is lost with the thousands on those careful, terrible lists.

Kevin Graham

PERENNIAL

Something about how short-lived the hour is
when fox cubs wake and moonlight spills
in grainy black and white. The day slips
and there's this irresistible song. Nothing holy,

just hope's crutch and a notable slack
in the tension. Happy to be alive to the moment
the sun leaves or separates or whatever
it's doing in the treetops across the river.

Something retreats and silence is restored.
Maybe time for the memory of a friend
in the wisp trailing from your cigarette.

Science talks in stages – civil, nautical,
astronomical – but they're more like ranges
drifting under wide, incredulous eyes.

FEATURED POET: ALVY CARRAGHER

Alvy Carragher was born in Galway. Describing her first years there she wrote: 'I went to one of those tiny country schools that city people find it hard to believe in.' Her undergraduate studies were in Lake Charles, Louisiana, where she had a sports scholarship. She returned to Dublin in 2012 and became part of the Dublin Writers' Forum, where she was able to develop a closer focus on her writing. She got her MA in Writing from University College Galway.

In 2016 her first book of poetry, *Falling in Love with Broken Things*, was published by Salmon Poetry. In an article in *The Irish Times* she characterized the themes of the work as 'about growing up in a world that is essentially broken, from natural disasters right down to our fundamental relationships'. She has also had a notable presence in the world of spoken word poetry, performing at many festivals. She has been a finalist in Slam competitions and has won other contests. As part of the 2016 Poetry Ireland Introductions readings, she represented the series at a reading at the Lincoln Center in New York.

The vivid, voice-driven poem featured here called 'the men I keep under my bed' – excerpted from a longer work – gestures to both page and performance. It is an extended persona piece, a dramatic narrative, voiced by a young woman on a morning run in the Phoenix Park. The narrative builds with the action: The speaker sets out in a pre-dawn, aware of the blur of headlights and the details of the morning. There are deer. A man practices Tai Chi between the trees – 'a strange place to be at peace', the runner notes. The landscape unfolds sometimes in lyric detail, at other times in staccato perceptions. But although the poem seems to move forward through free association, the deliberate and considered syntax and artful pacing unfolds a self, not just a situation. Finally the young woman returns home, to her empty sense of a one-night stand the previous night. The drama of the run fades and stasis returns.

Alvy Carragher's poem revisits a debate in contemporary poetry – a dialogue that often enough hasn't reached the status of that, but should. There are tensions and suspicions between page poetry and performance poetry: differences of allegiance and expectation. But all too often the suspicion of performance poetry in the world of traditional or academic poetry has missed the point. Performance poetry, slam poetry, is certainly committed to a voiced expression of the poem. But it can also uncover a rare energy too often lost on the page: a sure-footed transit by the oral poet towards public statement drawn out of private experience. In that process voice becomes not just an option, but a craft in itself. In the best circumstances, the poem that draws from voice and performance can migrate to the page, bringing those energies with it. Living in both dimensions with ease and confidence. As Alvy Carragher's poem does here.

– Eavan Boland

Alvy Carragher

THE MEN I KEEP UNDER MY BED

Note: the following is the opening section
of 'the men i keep under my bed'

out the door, down the stack of steps

September dark and street lights lead me along the North Circular Road
slow at first, easing myself into it,
limbs stiff and dissatisfied from lack of sleep

my runners slap the pavement
6am cars slug by in a blur of light
my breath is a cloud to run through

I argue

part of me would like to turn around
push my key into the lock, go back indoors
melt butter into toast, brew some coffee

(not the cheap kind, a man with coffee-snobbery sold it to me)

in that version of events, I do something wholesome
one of those activities Kasia suggested like yoga
she tutted when I told her about the running
bent over, her slight frame leaning forward
as she tapped my kneecap with her finger

what about your knees, are they not going to hurt

I shrugged, always the shrug
the half-answer to uncomfy questions
I rarely consider the fate of my knees
or any of the advice Kasia gives me, like

embrace the healing properties of yoghurt
or
a teaspoon of ascorbic acid per day

(keeps all sense of joy at bay)

two minutes into the run
Phoenix Park sits, white gates against the dark

I will myself to think like an apple
which is to *grow and be and fall*
I read it in some mindfulness book, that
and a chapter about pretending to be a seed

but I don't feel seed-like, they're all untapped potential
that's the kind of metaphor Mrs Ryan loved

compare yourself to fruit

a leaving cert English teacher's idea of poetry
then university professors go salivating over fertile pomegranates
until we're all products of poor metaphorical training

a stitch develops, nestled in my ribs, I slow
focus on filling up my lungs

half a mile into the park
the Garda Barracks to my back
I take the boring road
snake along the border walls
one flat line out to the trails
I save the hills for when I'm tired
for when the effort matters

11 minutes in, too soon to go back

when I run, I think of Scott Jurek
foot bandaged, suffering across Death Valley

I tried his technique before, shortening steps
increasing turnover, it felt treadmill heavy

(I should stop reading about Scott, he subsists on rice balls)

the length of a stride
feels like my body yawning across the ground
waking itself up

the grass that lines the road is wet and leaning
it smells like rain has been and rain is coming

I wear little glove skins
an old cotton race t-shirt, ratty leggings
the t-shirt has *I've been to Hell & Back* scrawled across it

(it feels silly or ironic
it's hard to differentiate)

if rain comes, cold will crawl into my lungs
make me into its home, spend weeks escaping from my nose
that's if I don't get gutted by a deer first, splatted by a car

I always scare myself with death

I'll run a little further
I don't want to deal with *him*
I'll have to ask *him* to leave
or make *him* breakfast
let *him* leave without a fuss

I'm good at pretending
smile, chit chat, then after *he* leaves
never reply to any texts *he* sends

(assuming *he*'s the sort to text)

I need to find *his* Facebook page, *he* must have one
that way I can check where *he*'s likely to show up
and avoid all those places

ah, this is my favourite bit
the dark is softer now
trees stretch toward the last chunk of moon

the moon will be gone
by the time I turn to go home
the sun will be coming up in front of me
its low-slung glow forcing me to watch the trail closely

I cross the back of the park
consider going further
but I can't miss the bus

it's best to act normal

people do this all the time, it's nothing to feel anything about
I need to stop being whimsical, me and my romantic notions

I'll veer here, loop through the wood
come out in front of the embassy
I love that stretchy piece of grass
it goes on for miles, deer skirt its edges

once a French woman stopped me
about half a mile into the park, she was desolate

they said there were deer, do you know where

I told her to keep going, they go wherever they feel like
she was wearing stupid shoes, I doubt she went any further
but you won't just stumble on beauty, it doesn't hang around waiting

maybe *he*'ll be gone by the time I get back
what was I thinking, I wasn't thinking, not really
is that a valid excuse for acting the mouldy slut

I push the thought back

it's not very feminist to consider myself a mouldy slut
I've agency over my body and all that 21st century shite

there's the road again
return across the trails or down the main road
that cuts through the centre of the park

I don't want to ruin the trail by associating it with this morning

I must be careful when I'm fragile
a subtle stump of wood
might stick in my subconscious

then months later
when I'm the new me
I'll take that trail
notice stumpy and
it will all come back

as if it never got put away

I'm being dramatic
this is, of course, grand

the road is spotted with the odd runner now

morning-time soul-searchers

cars slip into the city

I slow again, come close to stopping
the thud of dehydrated head hurt
I'll glug a pint of water, painkillers
recover from this ritual of pain

in six months, I've not learnt that
Dublin isn't kind

one glass becomes five
each glass a reminder that
I'm worn out by it all

it's okay for Sarah, Fridays start late for her
blundering out of bed at 11am
right about the time I slot into my desk
down my third coffee

it's hard to resist her, I tried

ah come on Beth
Diarmaid is driving me mad
would you not go for one
it'll do you good to get back out there

30 minutes, almost home

a man practices Tai Chi between the trees
a strange place to be at peace, so near the road
but I suppose the trick is finding peace there anyway

people can't seem to keep calmness to themselves
it seeps out of their pores, gets right up in my face
asks why I'm ticking over a thousand thoughts

up around the Polo Grounds
a runner strides on the other side of the grass

I pick the pace up, not slogging, not me
my stomach lumps at the new tempo

the tall thin loping figure goes by
I give him the runner's nod
once his footfalls are out of earshot
I slow to a waddle

I can't do this

the zoo's green fence holds in the sound of animals
their morning chorus, strangely haunting

how weak I am
the slower pace brings *him* back to me

I hope *he*'s not asleep
that *he* got up, slipped out, left no note
so, I can romanticise

what if

I hadn't gone running
left *him* slumped across my sheets

It's unsettling to watch a stranger sleeping
to feel their weight pressed along me in the bed
to see how vulnerable they can be in my presence
or how they reach towards me in their sleep
me or some memory of a girl they once loved
it is she they clutch at before waking

once awake
they realise she is gone

once awake
there is stilted conversation
or half-baked sex
to fill the not knowing
the mutual not wanting to know

this man was no sleep-reacher
not the sort to get hung up on hauntings
he was the nightmare of first attempts
rough and quick and rolled over

he left me wet and wanting

I didn't ask *him* to leave
I let *him* sleep

by morning, *his* light snore
took up all the room in my head

steady in the dark
I moved across the room
found my runners

now, I jog alongside the Barracks
a batch of Gardaí set out to run
the light is piecing the day together
people have that tired Friday slouch

I pass a uniformed girl with her mother
it seems sad that someone so young
is so perfectly pressed
her footsteps skip, bag jolting behind her

I should not be getting so down in the drudge
not wishing I could sleep all day Saturday

no sleep, it's Granny's birthday
I've to bus-haul home

Granny is eighty
one of those ages that seems impossible

imagine explaining to Granny that I've slept with a man
because I wanted to be held, but then *he* never held me

stop this, breathe, cop on

200 metres to the door
I need to quit moping
quit longing for boys that spoon
or have encyclopaedic knowledge
of topics I am ignorant in

I tried explaining to Sarah
about wanting someone fascinating

she asked

but like fascinating how

a butterfly enthusiast
someone who builds intricate watches
trains themselves to write the Japanese alphabet

Sarah says

that is the definition of being too fussy

I suspect the reality of a Japanese-writing butterfly enthusiast
would involve the kind of person who alphabetises their socks
sucks the last bit of chicken from the bone in a slurpy sound

creak of gate, I jog up the steps
fiddle with my keys at the door
try to remember *his* name
perhaps I'll need to use it

was *he* a Conor or maybe an accountant
I associate accountants with bland names

(if you name a baby Conor
you might as well sign them up
for spreadsheets in the womb)

I push open the door
the hall is the dark of rest

I pause, before entering

Danny Sheehy

MARGAÍ FALSA

Níor thuigeas riamh,
ní thuigim fós,
ní thuigfeadh choíche
ná ní theastaíonn uaim a thuiscint;
Footsie, Iseq Overall Index, Dow Jones,
sell off of equities, financial centres,
stocmhargadh, scarannaí, stocbhannaí,
margadh na hÉireann síos trí fén gcéad,
trádáil, margaíocht, díol agus ceannach
ar mhargaí falsa an domhain mhóir.
Conas a thuigfinn a leithéid
mar ní chím éinní á dhíol ná á cheannach
ach fuirse is fuadar is fotharaga
fé thaibhsí i gculaitheanna síoda.
Is deas é an tine agus rud le n-ithe.

N'fheadair cá bhfuil Wall Street,
Hong Kong ná Singapore ach
tá fhios agam cá bhfhuil
Sliabh Bhaile an Chalaidh
Portach an Fhearainn, An Leacain,
Newcastle, Sheffield, Ford's Dagenham
agus an Meánoirthear
mar is as na háiteanna san
a fuaireas agus a gheibhim
móin agus gual don dtine,
forc agus scian chun greim
a chur i mo bhéal,
díosail agus peitril chun fuinneamh
a ghiniúint i gcairteacha
a bheireann mé ó cheann ceann na tíre.
Is deas é an tine agus rud le n-ithe.

Cad is fiú dom eolas a chur ar Wall Street
mar níl le fáil ann práta síl ná scailliún inniún.
Chuireas eolas dom ainneoin ar Canary Warf
mar ar chuir buama diamhaireach an IRA
smidiríní uafáis ag rás trí aigne plánálta na dtaibhsí síodúla.
Is deas é an tine agus rud le n-ithe.

Cad chuige an deabhadh atá ar an Dow Jones?
Canathaobh go bhfhuil oiread éilimh
ar na margaí áiféiseacha seo mar
ní bhfaighir iontu greim bídh ná galún oíle
ach iad falsa fealltach scannrúil bréagach.
Samhlaítear dom go bhfuil an slua sí
i gcumhacht is ag imirt cleasa,
draíocht, cur i géill is cearrbhachas
ar bhaothstoc damanta an tsaoil
ag bualadh poc ar imreas focal
ag creimeadh cladaigh is cóstaí
ag loscadh an aeir is na spéireach
is ag milleadóireacht ar phobal Dé.
Is deas é an tine agus rud le n-ithe.

Ná bacaimis le trádáil domhanda
ach fuineadh de réir na mine,
comhar na gcomharsan,
pobail áitiúla agus meithealacha oibre.
Díol is ceannaigh is babhtáil de réir do mhéin
is tabhair leat abhaile mar a oirfidh duit.
Tá gach ní inár dtimpeall a thugann dúinn
oíche chodlata, sláinte, bolg lán,
tine, teas agus greim inár mbéalaibh.
Is deas é an tine agus rud le n-ithe.

Peter Sirr

STONE MAD

Richard Murphy, *In Search of Poetry* (Clutag Press, 2017), £15.

What is the cost of poetry? Or rather, what is the cost to oneself and others of a life of dedication to a lonely art? Which perfection, in the Yeatsian formula, do you choose, the life or the work? The title of Richard Murphy's new book suggests a reflection on the art of poetry from a master practitioner who has just celebrated his ninetieth birthday, but the book is much more personal and intimate than that. Part journal, part working diary, part memoir, all from the early 1980s and sections of which were originally published in *Poetry Ireland Review,* it charts the initiation and development of the sonnet sequence that would make up *The Price of Stone*, the poet's much praised 1985 collection. Each poem, in what became a fifty sonnet sequence, ventriloquises a building that has a resonance for the poet. This in turn means that the poet becomes the addressee, the biographical subject matter displaced into the consciousness of a roof-tree, restaurant, industrial school, or ancestral home. The poems are free to address and accuse the poet so that the sequence also functions as an oblique self-examination. 'By making the persona of each sonnet the spirit of that house or structure,' the poet said in a recent interview, 'I found I was better able to transmute the mud of remembered experience into urns of poetry'.

In these poems, Murphy's is a mind in search of strategies to protect itself against its own privacy. Abhorring any sort of direct revelation or confessionalism, he can let his buildings do the dirty conscience work for him. Dennis O'Driscoll, who was an important confidant and mentor, well understood this aspect of Murphy:

> Dennis O'Driscoll ... tells me on the phone that giving voice to a symbolic building, such as 'Folly' and 'Lead Mine Chimney', is a break-through from the stagnation and mental blocks that have often afflicted me ... he says these sonnets reveal more about myself in a less embarrassing way than poems written in my own voice.

The sonnets are a strange, and strangely effective achievement: cool, orderly, 'in granite style', seemingly remote yet full of quiet surprises, rhyming 'firmament' and 'ferment' but also 'steam' and 'jism', and ranging over a wide terrain, from the intimate to the declamatory, the pompous swagger to the bleak cruelty of Letterfrack Industrial School. Murphy describes here the often difficult quest for the precise verbal effect, trawling through the OED to find, for 'Portico', the word 'cineritious' (ash-coloured), with 'connotations of "sin" and "penitence" ', or 'succursal' (a subsidiary cell of a church or monastery), or 'ithyphallus' for an 'erect phallus'. There is, in the notes as much as in the poems, that careful sense of foraging, weighing, considering, until each poem's construction is locked down.

The poems here also, inevitably, interrogate his own origins. A Murphy ancestor would have been the first to 'take the soup', starting a journey from peasant impoverishment to the patrician reaches of Anglo-Irishness and his father's career as colonial governor of the Bahamas and Ceylon, where he was the last British mayor of Columbo. Murphy locates his own voice partly in the change from Irish to English – a change also of tradition, culture and religion – which left him 'the voice with which I speak and write ... a voice that hungers for authority and yearns to make people and things, which are sure to vanish, last in verbal granite'. A poem like 'Carlow Village Schoolhouse' allows him to see an Anglicanized forebear in his forbidding school, caning a pupil for speaking Irish, and asks:

> Not forced to sip
> The cauldron soup with undying gratitude,
> Would *you* have chosen to board a coffin-ship?

Unease is at the heart of the poems, as well as the entries here. Murphy is never really at home, whether in his 'new suburban Catholic Irish nationalist neighbourhood', his own history, or his own immediate family. He seeks refuge instead in the dramatic land and seascapes of the West, in grand male pursuits of sailing, farming, or obsessive building projects, realising that his renovations – really another kind of solitariness – were in fact often as much an escape from responsibilities as an addition to family life.

Often this kind of realisation comes too late, of course. Twenty years after his divorce from his first wife, and after her death, he reads for the first time Pascal's *Pensées*, one of her favourite books: 'This has made me realise with remorse how deeply my hunger to acquire and improve more land and buildings hurt her.' His greatest refuge, though, is in the slow, painstaking crafting of poems, and this is the book's real focus. The lines are agonised over, written and rewritten. Dennis O'Driscoll's reactions are solicited, and Murphy's reports of their conversations provide a fascinating insight into how the negotiation between private creation and valued audience provided a space where his art could flourish. When he gets stuck, Dennis is on hand with sound advice:

> Knocked off the surf-board, how long it takes to rise and balance on another wave. 'Write the interruptions into the poetry,' Dennis advises on the phone, 'or at least into the notebook.' Let the sequence grow to three dozen, or whatever number of sonnets gives a sense of fulfilment.

As well as filling in many of the personal blanks the poems keep to themselves, these journals record the constant struggle to keep poems alive. The poet, fittingly in this context, always sounds like an architect or a builder about to get his hands dirty: 'I am about to begin work on the construction of a new poem about the reclamation of a old building ...' The book, a very useful addition to the Murphy corpus, ends where it began, in Knockbrack, the Killiney house Murphy bought and renovated, with the poet sitting at his table and trying, as always, 'to build a poem that will be beyond repair'.

Aoife Lyall

NITA, SRI LANKA, 2005

You pet her coarse mitten hands.
Pinch her stitched toes.
Pat her cotton hair.

'Nita', sewn neatly onto her modest vest.
In Hebrew, it means *Grace*; in Indian *faithful*.
Native American, *bear*.
(That's what we call you).

Taller than you,
you look up to her and laugh
at her dark eyes, her curved nose,
her thin red-stitched smile.

She is twelve years old now;
one of twelve thousand made
for the twelve thousand lost.

Your first doll, you will give her
the thoughts and words the tsunami
washed away. You will give her life,
never knowing she has died.

John O'Donnell

THE LUCAS PLANET NO. 33

i.m. Seamus Heaney

I

Say first a sup of kerosene, poured deftly into the squat casing
at the base, and then a match scratched into action, held flare-headed,
steady-handed in the opened porthole, your other hand turning
the handle so that the wick rose like a cobra charmed to greet
the flame, the enamelled blackness of the chamber suddenly aglow
in its own solstice. The cover then snapped shut, the spring-hinge
bracket-clipped beneath the handlebars and you're off,
a leg swung easy over the saddle, your wavering front beam
diminishing the evening lengthening between us until you disappear.

II

Then say another oil, a different kind of light:
sweet balm of chrism and the spear-tipped flames of candles,
white flowers hushing the room, and you in your good suit,
as ready as you can be for the journey, the ditches lined
with curious schoolchildren and stout policemen saluting as you pass
on your way north to where we lay you down between sycamore and ash,
low prayers and beak-twitter and murmured choked goodbyes,
and afterwards the hydraulic stutter of the digger,
its swung bucket a hero's empty helmet, scooping up and filling in
the opened ground; a lifetime's earth.

III

But now the way ahead is unlit, unapproved; no knowing
what may come hurtling without warning from the hedgerows,
oblivion in wait behind each trembling leaf, and nothing equal
to the darkness of this grief except perhaps the Lucas Planet No. 33,
the long-gone manufacturer's proud boast emblazoned on the box it comes in:
'We make light of our labours', and for a moment the world is once more lit
by the power-surge of your grin, delighting in the pun, and crediting as well
the credo of all art: to make the effort made seem effortless while going
to the heart of what matters. Actual and emblem, this venerable bicycle-lamp;
sturdy, trustworthy, the heft of it a kind of grace, and this time I take off,
unsteadily; still sad, and fearful, yes: uncertain where I'm going
but gladdened by this ghost-light, the road before me brightening
in its occult and familiar gleam. Wheel-spin; spoke-song.
The consolation that what's well-made endures, and shines on.

Tomás de Faoite

BOTANIST

A botanist told me at my father's wake
that the poet Séamus Dall Mac Cuarta was
buried in the same graveyard as my family.
Someone remarked: "Your father looks well."
The botanist said: "No better than he did
yesterday, when he was still alive, a bit paler."
The room silenced, no one spoke, people
stilled. I looked at my father; sure
he was paler, off colour like elder berry
blossom that can be turned into a potion
to set the mind free and wild for
an hour or two. But what we were left with
was an awkwardness, a brute zen-moment
of absolute fact. He was gone
not here, not there, just gone
into what was beyond us, non-being,
his consciousness uploaded like a bird in the trees
who sings the beauty of shrubs to the sun.

Paddy Bushe

FAMILY MEAL

Again, the same dream. He's outside
The window of his own house.
Again he has locked himself out.

There is a table, pooled in light.
There is a family, an evening meal.
There is a woman, a boy, a girl

Facing the silhouette of a man
Whose unlit back is to the window.
The girl stares towards both men,

Sees only the man in the room. The man
Outside does not recognise the dark
Bulk of the man the girl watches

In the lamplight. Nor can he hear
Anything she says across the table
Or any answer the man may make.

The rigid smile she hides behind
Shows nothing of the icy shards
He feels encircle her heart and eyes.

He knows it well now, this dream
Where he has locked himself outside.
Years and years too late he beats

At window glass that will not shatter
But echoes dully like hammered
Lead weights around his guilty heart.

Killian O'Donnell

THE GIVEN

Six months in, we're old news: no longer
shot past on the Carna-Cashel road without a beep of recognition
that acknowledges our presence
in the scheme of things – except by nervy tourists –

and just beginning to exchange
the formal courtesies of small talk in Supervalu on the price
of everything in Lidl for a kind of hedged warmth,
a curiosity that has us adding our twist to the flurries of opinion

on the new weirdness
of the weather, the perennial me-féinery of politicians,
the price of greed. And even if
we are still blow-ins – and granted

that's a field we'll be picking stones out of for the rest of our lives
here – it's starting to feel normal
to be shaken by sunsets, less wrongfooted by the gorse
that won't stop growing, and be glad, as we slow

to a crawl on the home-stretch from Johnnie's
through spring tides of darkness visible, dicky foglights bouncing off
the curtained windows of the cottages
of the summer-people, to find the light in our house a given.

Eavan Boland

PATRICK KAVANAGH: FIFTY YEARS ON

Patrick Kavanagh died fifty years ago. His name has rarely been absent from comment and controversy since then. In his lifetime he could be scathing and colourful in speech: he wrote prose that pilloried the sacred cows of a city and an establishment, whoever or whatever they happened to be at that moment. As a defence his enemies portrayed him as oafish in manner and ungrateful by disposition.

I had the good fortune to meet Kavanagh when I was still a student. I sat across from him in a café at the bottom of Grafton Street, where they still turned and gritted the coffee beans in the window. Our conversation was brief but memorable, at least for me. And yet it would be years before I could unpick the legendary threads, the second-hand mythology of the poet. Once I did I could bring with me into later life not an image of sitting across from him, but the less easily realized shape of a writer of persistence and craft: an innovative and dissenting poet, neither afraid of the limits of his subject matter nor the reach of his own imagination.

Patrick Kavanagh was born in the border county of Monaghan, in the townland of Inniskeen, in 1904. He described his father as 'a shoemaker, small farmer, hob doctor and ditto lawyer'. The farm was less than forty acres. But despite the hard-pressed times, the lack of money, the claustrophobia, Kavanagh kept a passionate attachment to his birthplace. 'There are several fields I long to see again', he wrote later. All his life, the best of his poetry and prose would evoke the ditches, crossroads, frosty vistas, and remembered visions of his birthplace.

Kavanagh was an unswerving critic of the Irish Revival. 'It is usually taken for granted', he wrote in an article, 'that there was a great literary renaissance in Ireland within the last fifty years. How little of all that writing was of the slightest merit!'

He came to Dublin in 1939 and lived there from then on, despite being a reluctant city-dweller. He wrote and published poetry, much of it an implicit critique of the nationalism and idealism of the Revival. One of his most ambitious poems, 'The Great Hunger', was published in the British magazine *Horizon* in 1942, and brought out as a Cuala Press pamphlet by Frank O'Connor in the same year. It was a scalding anti-pastoral, a testament to a confined life and a wounded sexuality.

In some of his later comments, Kavanagh explained his resistance to the Revival. 'When I came to Dublin', he wrote, 'the Irish Literary Affair was still booming. It was the notion that Dublin was a literary metropolis and Ireland, as invented and patented by Yeats, Lady Gregory and Synge, a spiritual entity. It was full of writers and poets and I am afraid I thought their work had the Irish quality.'

His comments, indeed his entire attitude, suggested a suspicion that he himself might be screen-tested by the Revival to become a laureate of tragic rusticity. 'Had I stuck to the tragic thing in The Great Hunger', he wrote, 'I would have found many powerful friends.' He moved on. Throughout the forties and fifties his poems grew shorter, more visionary, more dissident. The early social comment was burned away and what emerged were poems of deep private displacement.

Kavanagh has now entered the history of Irish literature in a more settled way. With retrospect, his questions seem more justified and his achievement more remarkable. He is also better served by critics now than he once was. There is a fine biography of him by Antoinette Quinn. But his true posthumous luck lies in his starring role in a beautiful, wrenching book. It is called *Dead as Doornails*. It was written by Anthony Cronin, and was first published in 1976.

Dead as Doornails is an account of post-war literary Dublin. The three writers observed are Brendan Behan, Flann O'Brien, and Patrick Kavanagh. Their daily existence, their deep frustrations with lack of money and opportunity, their impatience with convention – all are recorded. I have never read a better or more complex elegy for writers and the way they lived. I doubt there is one. Not that the book is sentimental. The writers who walk through the pages are unswervingly described. But they are never the villains. If there is a villain it is that period of Irish literary life – that time of shadows, shortages, and hardships. The actual writers, as described by Cronin, light up the pages. They speak, protest, and gesture in powerful and surprising prose. Anthony Cronin, as well as being a distinguished poet, was a superb man of letters. He not only records these lives. He mourns the circumstances that constrained gifted men and with a rare eloquence. Among those circumstances were the tabloid simplifications of their lives in their own moment. Cronin references this with regard to Kavanagh:

> The town it is true buzzed with stories of his sayings and his behaviour, but they were stories designed to show him as a maladroit, mannerless oaf, and among the sort of people who retailed them, even the now very cursory acknowledgements of genius were left out. One heard such sto-

> ries everywhere. They were part of Dublin's social currency. If the person concerned was literary, he might just gravely incline his head and say, It was a pity Paddy hadn't stayed down on the farm and stuck to the lyric thing, that he was making a fool out of himself in Dublin and it wasn't doing him any good.

The cruelty and disrespect of such remarks are a common thread in *Dead as Doornails*. They remind us of a time when the acceptance of writers was more limited in Ireland than anyone now would believe. Which makes Cronin's account even more valuable. When he finally meets Kavanagh in person, something different happens. It is one of the great strengths of *Dead as Doornails* that Cronin is able to offer a different impression to us and to all the futures in which Kavanagh will continue to exist:

> It therefore came as something of a surprise to me, when I met him through *Envoy*, to find that Patrick Kavanagh was a deeply serious man with an intellect which was humorous and agile, as well as being profound and apparently incorruptible. He was also, in that first relationship at least, apparently warm and generous. On someone who already admired his work, his impact was extraordinary. More than any other man I have met, he fitted Dr Johnson's description of Edmund Burke: 'If you sheltered with him in a doorway from a drove of oxen for a minute, you would depart from him knowing you had been in the company of a man of genius.'

It is that 'deeply serious man' this half-century anniversary allows us to consider. It is that Kavanagh I want to remember here. He has seemed to me not only a signature writer of the Irish twentieth century, but something more as well: a figure creating a revelatory momentum within Irish poetry, and – wider than that – the history of poetry. But the context for all this requires a small detour ...

In 1977 the Nigerian writer Chinua Achebe published an article in the *Massachusetts Review*. It was called 'An Image of Africa: Racism in Conrad's "Heart of Darkness"'. It had previously been given as a lecture in Amherst in 1975, when Achebe was visiting there. The Black Atlantic writer Caryl Phillips described the lecture 'as one of the most important and influential treatises in post-colonial literary discourse'.

The argument of Achebe's piece was a passionate and clarifying denunciation of the way Joseph Conrad represented African figures and Africanness itself in his novella. Conrad's book tracks the journey of Marlow, a sailor, as he navigates the Congo river. But it is not the plot that disturbs Achebe. It is Conrad's mindset. He holds him responsible for the misrepresentations of Africa he sees in the book, refusing to accept they belong – as some have argued – to his protagonist. 'Conrad appears to go to considerable pains to set up layers of insulation between himself and the moral universe of his history', Achebe states. Conrad therefore, in Achebe's view is fully responsible and no arguments that this is fiction can exempt him from that responsibility.

The lecture makes it clear that to Achebe it is intolerable that the honours and titles of art should be granted to a text that he considers demeaning to his own countrymen. Defending his argument and anticipating criticism he writes: 'There are two probable grounds on which what I have said so far may be contested. The first is that it is no concern of fiction to please people about whom it is written. I will go along with that. But I am not talking about pleasing people. I am talking about a book which parades ... prejudices and insults from which a section of mankind has suffered untold agonies.'

Chinua Achebe's article opened decades of debate. Conrad's defenders and Achebe's supporters found little common ground. But one thing remained undeniable: whatever side of the argument was taken, Achebe's luminous anger and ethical concerns were clearly of immense importance. His argument to this day remains deeply moving. But the reason I quote from it here is not because of Conrad or *Heart of Darkness.* It is because the meaning of Achebe's argument goes beyond a single fiction. It raises a further question that he himself embodies: What happens when an individual or a people who have been simplified or demeaned – as Achebe sees it – will no longer hold still within the literature that does this to them? What happens when a person once objectified in that literature walks out of those tropes and becomes an author, able to shift and change what once held them in stasis? What, in summary, happens when the objects of a literature become the authors of it? What is the nature of that journey? And how can we track it? Those are the questions I want to apply to Kavanagh. Some of the answers – large as the questions are – may be partially suggested by this micro-focus:

In 1951 Kavanagh published a sonnet in *The Bell Magazine*. It was called 'Epic', and became a celebrated instance of his work. The poem appeared at the start of a new decade – the years indeed covered by Anthony Cronin in *Dead as Doornails*:

Epic

I have lived in important places, times
When great events were decided, who owned
That half a rood of rock, a no-man's land

Surrounded by our pitchfork-armed claims.
I heard the Duffys shouting 'Damn your soul'
And old McCabe stripped to the waist, seen
Step the plot defying blue cast-steel –
'Here is the march along these iron stones.'
That was the year of the Munich bother. Which
Was more important? I inclined
To lose my faith in Ballyrush and Gortin
Till Homer's ghost came whispering to my mind.
He said: I made the *Iliad* from such
A local row. Gods make their own importance.

The poise and satire here, the subversive juxtaposition of a private rural quarrel with a seismic historic event, show Kavanagh's true grace of artistry. He was uniquely equipped with his clean, bold syntax, his sharp contrasting of talky lines with oracular ones, to create a rare vernacular space. But the poem shows something else as well. In many ways it was stranded in its moment. The 'Munich bother' referred to by the poem had happened years earlier. Now the war was over and 1951 was itself an odd year, full of maverick and disconnected events in Ireland: Ernest Walton won the Nobel Prize in Physics. The Abbey theatre burned to the ground. And Samuel Beckett published *Molloy*, but in French.

None of those events contextualize 'Epic'. To get a real context for the poem we need to travel back almost thirteen years. The British scholar Jon Stallworthy tells us in an article in the *Review of English Studies* in 1966 that the first draft of one of Yeats's final poems, 'Under Ben Bulben', was being made ready in August 1938 .It was completed over the next few months. On 26 January 1939, Yeats gave the poem to his wife with final corrections. He died at 2 p.m. two days later on 28 January 1939. Sometime between the August of 1938 and the January of 1939 he completed the final part of the poem with these well known lines:

Irish poets, learn your trade,
Sing whatever is well made,
Scorn the sort now growing up
All out of shape from toe to top,
Their unremembering hearts and heads
Base-born products of base beds.
Sing the peasantry, and then
Hard-riding country gentlemen,
The holiness of monks, and after
Porter-drinkers' randy laughter;
Sing the lords and ladies gay

That were beaten into the clay
Through seven heroic centuries;
Cast your mind on other days
That we in coming days may be
Still the indomitable Irishry.

How are we to read the relation between these two poems – between Yeats's legacy statement and Kavanagh's *Ars Poetica*? I think we should see that relation as showing up a kind of artistic disruption, one which the Irish Revival for all its strengths simply never considered. That disruption happens when the objects of a literature become the authors of it. Nor is it only a matter of representation. The poem that objectifies a rural world – as Yeats does in 'Under Ben Bulben' – as well as those who live there not only runs the risk of simplifying those subjects, but also of silencing them. Therefore when those ghosts of silence begin to speak for themselves, an intense and proper disruption takes place.

And this is what is happening here. Looking at the end of 'Under Ben Bulben', it's plain that Kavanagh's name is not written there: that Yeats's poem represents in Adrienne Rich's phrase 'A book of myths in which our names do not appear'. Instead of new names, what's on offer is Yeats's design for a stratified Ireland. In that sense, with its stage directions for future Irish poets – *sing the peasantry* – the lines don't just simplify the subject, they erase it.

Yeats did many great things. This is not one of them. The journey from 'Under Ben Bulben' to 'Epic' therefore had to be undertaken as the arduous imaginative transit of a single poet, subverting everything from Irish history to the sonnet form with his own authorship. But that individual journey also encodes the journey of a society – of an Irish people who could no longer see themselves in the mirror of the hierarchy Yeats proposes. In undertaking that migration from object to author Kavanagh, who could not find his name uttered by his precursors, wrote a new name and a new poetry.

On this fiftieth anniversary of his death, there are many reasons to celebrate and remember Patrick Kavanagh. First and foremost, for his beautiful, plain-speaking poems with their powerful complications and formal sense of adventure – as in the Canal Bank sonnets. But for something else as well. In his journey into his own space, Kavanagh gave a radical and influential witness of the poet's independence from tradition and objectification. Like his poems, that influence, that witness, remains – still making and remaking a future for Irish poetry.

Ben McGuire

WILD APPLE

The Lyman alpha forest is an absorption phenomenon seen in the spectra of (especially distant) high redshift quasars and galaxies. It is the only direct observational evidence we have of the existence and properties of the general intergalactic medium.

– Michael Rauch

Wild apple of our eye, hung
crimson in the Lyman alpha forest that grew round you,

tangle of theorized light absorption,
        loop in a net
cast
      over space –
apple,
dark matter,
concept, unmet friend,

to us you are
what you are,
        part of everything.

Deirdre Daly

SPRAWL

I trace your boundaries as we lounge on a quilt,
a spread of threadbare blooms. Frontiers reclaimed

by pure Americana. Our names are lost in new suburbs,
hushed by construction sites, cut by the hum of a motorway.

Workers scratch the dirt, dumping rock, not of shrines,
but polished verandas to one side as Ireland's new villages

no longer need churches. Their hollering pierces the heavy air,
sneaks into the bedroom through the open window. No mind,

we are drunk still on the sticky inertia of Dublin in July.
Dusk and the settling dust is mahogany. Against the light

our bed of cotton flowers burns beneath us. Your sounds
are the call of the earliest thrush, a stream's roll, the grind

of rock, the first flap of a wing. Our voices coax
a nocturne from the corners of the room. We answer the question

of a hymn by cracking rafters, splitting plaster walls,
ripping the ceiling and breaking double-glazed glass.

Nowhere else to be, but right here.
We have our song. We are without the need of prayer.

Mary Montague

THE OPPOSITE BIRDS

after Dyke and Kaiser

Dead languages translate
Mesozoic runes into a precise
vocabulary that powers
the enantiornithes

back into the air
on their alternatively
arranged bones
of the pectoral girdle

whereby a boss
on the coracoid
articulated with a facet
on the scapula, unlike

modern birds where
a boss on the scapula
articulates with a facet
on the coracoid.

But, overlooking
the teeth, the clawed manus,
in other respects the opposites
were the same: wing proportions

were of a volant bird; a triosseal
pulley system worked
the shoulder; the carina
plunged for massive

attachment of muscle;
and the furcula
was narrow and slender
as any wishbone that springs

to assist the flight stroke
for long migrations
across the new oceans
of the Cretaceous

or flitting through forests
of cycad. Where they thrived.
All that's left are featherings
petrified in volcanic ash

to conjure words – marks
on our perishable artefacts –
quickening the breath at a rush
of alternative wings.

Alan Titley

IDIR DHÁ AIGNE

Louis de Paor (eagarthóir), *Leabhar na hAthghabhála/Poems of Repossession: 20th-century poetry in Irish*, Irish-English bilingual edition (Cló Iar-Chonnacht/ Bloodaxe Books, 2016), €20 / £15.

Ní foláir nó tá sé ar cheann de na saothair is mó contúirt i saol na litríochta, díolaim a chur le chéile. Pé rud is a dhéanfaidh tú, beifear ann a bheidh thar a bheith míshásta léi. Na dlúthchairde is fearr atá agat, b'fhéidir go dtabharfá gramhas áirithe ar a bpus faoi deara agus iad i gcomhrá caoin leat; agus chaithfeá a bheith ag féachaint thar do ghualainn agus tú ag triall abhaile tar éis ócáidí áirithe liteartha ar eagla na scine sa droim nó an chloch sa mhuinchille. Is mó is contúirtí an bheart nuair atá go leor de na scríbhneoirí beo, agus cuid acu beithíoch agus ag faire amach duit. Tugadh cuireadh dom féin díolaim d'fhilíocht na Nua-Ghaeilge a thiomsú tá suim bhlianta ó shin ann, ach dhiúltaigh mé toisc gur thuigeas go mbeadh mo bhreithiúntas féin ar imeall na slí, ach níos tromchúisí ná sin, gur theastaigh uaim a raibh de chairde na héigse agam a choimeád.

Dá réir sin, is misniúil an mhaise do Louis de Paor an leabhar tomadach mór seo a chur le chéile is a mbíonn de bhobghaistí ar feadh an bhóthair. Tá de bhuntáiste aige, áfach, go bhfuil aidhm éagsúil go maith ag an mbailiúchán seo seachas na cinn a chuaigh roimhe. Áirím ar a laghad deich gcinn de chnuasaigh nua-fhilíochta ó aimsir sraith sin *Nua-fhilí* Shéamais Uí Chéileachair, nó *Duanaire Nua-fhilíochta* Frank O'Brien féin anuas go dtí, abraimis, *Fearann Pinn* Ghréagóra Uí Dhúill. Chuir mé mac léinn iarchéime aon uair amháin ag obair ar na díolaimí seo féachaint arbh fhéidir aon 'chanóin' nua-fhilíochta a fháscadh astu. Ba de shuimiúlacht gurbh é a thátal, fág beagán éigin a fuair bheith istigh sna díolaimí scoile as an áireamh, nárbh fhéidir. Is é sin le rá, an bhfuil aon duine againn, idir scoláirí agus chriticeoirí agus fhilí agus ghnáthléitheoirí féin, an bhfuil aon duine againn aontaithe ar chritéir agus ar shlata tomhais an fheabhsa agus na dearscnaitheachta? Ní móide go bhfuil.

Ní dhéanann Louis de Paor aon éileamh ar chanóin a shocrú ná a dhaingniú leis an leabhar seo, cé gur dócha gur céim chun na críche sin is ea gach díolaim ina bealach féin. Is é is cuspóir dó scoth na filíochta nua-aimseartha a chur ar fáil 'for readers of English who do not otherwise have access to material in Irish, and for those with some knowledge of the language who may find the English versions helpful as a bridge towards a fuller engagement with 20th-century poetry in Irish.' Tá an méid sin soiléir.

Bhí díolaimí roimhe seo ann, gan amhras, inar féachadh le haistriúcháin a chur le hais na mbundánta. Cuimhním go háirithe ar *An Crann faoi Bhláth/The Flowering Tree* le Declan Kiberd and Gabriel Fitzmauirice, agus ar *An Tonn Gheal/The Bright Wave* a chuir Dermot Bolger in eagar. Tá an leabhar seo i bhfad níos iomláine agus níos cuimsithí ná aon cheann díobh sin, agus dá réir sin, clúdaíonn an fearann le fairsingeacht. Cuirtear prionsabal eile os ár gcomhair maidir le leagan amach na bhfilí. In ionad iad a chur i láthair de réir aoise nó de réir litreacha na haibítre féin 'the poets appear in sequence according to the year in which their debut collections were published.' Is chuige seo, ionas go bhfeicfear an anáil a bhí acu ar a chéile, má bhí, agus craobhú na filíochta féin i ngan fhios dúinn ag an am. Sílim gur prionsabal ar fónamh é sin, cé go bhfuil cead ag gach eagarthóir gabháil don ábhar ina shlí féin. Ba shainiúil ar fad, mar shampla, an ciúta a tharraing Ciarán Ó Coigligh chuige féin ina dhíolaim *An Fhilíocht Chomhaimseartha* 1975-1985. Is amhlaidh gur roghnaigh sé na dánta ab fhearr, dar leis, ó na cnuasaigh éagsúla a foilsíodh le linn thréimhse an leabhair ionas go bhfeicfeá leithne na héigse go follas ach go mba dheacra gaisce nó fás aon fhile ar bith a rianadh le haon chruinneas.

Mo thuairim féin nach bhfuil sé cothrom ná bailí rogha eagarthóra a lochtú. Sin é pribhléid an té a rinne. Muran maith leat é, cuirtear do chnuasach féin in eagar!

Tá an t-eagarthóir i gcónaí ag siúl ar imeall na faille sin idir ceart a thabhairt don phictiúr mór ar leith amháin, agus ceart a thabhairt do dhánta aonair den scoth ar an leith eile. An ann don chnuasach go díreach ar son pléisiúir aeistéitiúil na léitheoireachta a thabhairt dúinn is cuma cad as nó cén seasamh atá ag an aiste filíochta, nó an bhfuil dualgas níos leithne air an pictiúr mór a dhearadh agus gluaiseacht scuabach na litríochta seo a léiriú dúinn ina lánfhuinneamh? Arís eile ar ais, ní dóigh liom go bhfuil aon réiteach simplí air seo agus caithfear dul le rogha an eagarthóra agus a bhfuil curtha aige inár láthair. Níl ach beirt sa chnuasach nach bhfuil ach aon dán amháin acu ann, mar atá, Pádraig Ó hÉigeartaigh agus Seán Ó Curraoin; agus i gcás an Churraoinigh is sliocht as dán fada fiorshainiúil atá ann. Is léir, mar sin, gur shocraigh Louis de Paor ar rogha fhilí chomh maith le rogha dánta a chur ar fáil.

Is ea, leis, braithfidh daoine uathu dánta a bhí coitianta go maith sna cnuasaigh mheánscoile le Caoimhín Ó Conghaile, mar shampla, nó le Séamas Ó Céileachair, hArt Ó Maolfabhail, Seán Ó hÉigeartaigh, Réamann Ó Muireadhaigh, Seán Mac Fheorais, Micheál Mac Liammóir, Tomás Tóibín, Pearse Hutchinson agus eile, agus cá bhfuil Breandán Ó Beacháin féin lena dhá dhán den scoth? An amhlaidh go bhfuil leathcheal déanta ar an idirghlúin sin gur tháinig ann dóibh ó réabhlóid an Direáin-ríordánaigh agus muintir INNTI agus ar lean iad? Bhíodh frása ag sonadh im chluasa féin ó Denis Donoghue a raibh sé de mhí-ádh liom freastal ar chuid dá léachtaí; ba mhinic é ag caint ar fhilí go raibh 'achieved oeuvre' acu, is é sin, daoine a chaith dúthracht saoil leis an ngairm acu agus nach raibh a seasamh ar aon splanc iontach amháin, dá fheabhas. D'fhan an frása liom, mar tá dealramh leis. Ar éigean teora leis na filí sin a bhfuil dán nó dornán dánta den chéadghrád amach thuas a bhainfeadh an cloigeann de na haingil féin, ach níor chuige sin an cnuasach seo, ná baol air. Tá filí ar lár anseo a bhfuil an 'achieved oeuvre' sin acu, smaoiním ar Ghréagóir Ó Dúill agus ar Art Ó Maolfabhail go háirithe, ach sin é nádúr an chúrsa agus sa chás is go bhfuil cnuasach 'gabhálach', ní féidir leis a bheith 'idirghabhálach' ar fad. Tá, leis, ar lár, duine de na filí is suimiúla agus is grinne samhlaíochta agus duine a choinnigh a shúil ar an domhan mór ag tabhairt gaotha móra an domhain isteach chugainn, agus is é sin Gabriel Rosenstock. Tuigim, áfach, gur dá dheoin féin a fágadh amuigh é, agus is trua mar sin ba ghá a bheith.

Beidh uimhirchloigne an chomhairimh amuigh ina choinne chomh maith. Líon na ndaoine ó na canúintí éagsúla, líon na mban is na bhfear, líon na ndánta le cách, líon na línte féin. Tá an t-áireamh déanta agam, mar uaireanta bím mar sin i ndoircheántacht na hoíche istigh. Ní fiú scaoinse an áirseora é. Muran maith leat é, mar adúirt cheana, cum agus ceap agus cnuasaigh do dhíolaim féin!

Is léir ar leagan amach an leabhair – agus tá creidiúint an-mhór ag dul do Chló Iar-Chonnacht agus do Bhloodaxe araon ar earra álainn inláimhsithe inléite a chur ar fáil in ainneoin toirte – go bhfuil aidhm léirmhínithe aige. Fara an réamhrá sholéite, tá nótaí tuisceanacha ar go leor de na dánta ar chúl an leabhair. Ní nótaí don mhac léinn iad seo, ach eolas leordhóthanach ar son roinnt de na poncanna dorcha, nó tagairtí cultúir a shoilsiú: abraimis 'cranna foirtil' Mháirtín Uí Dhireáin, nó 'feis' Nuala Ní Dhomhnaill, nó téarmaí Laidne Eoghain Uí Thuairisc in 'Aifreann na Marbh'. Níl slabhraí troma ar bith ar sileadh uathu ach miniúcháin a shaibhríonn an léitheoireacht oiread is gátar.

Ar an gcuma chéanna tá ailt ghearra ó chuid de na haistritheoirí ar an gceird nó ar an tuiscint a bhí acu agus iad i mbun a gcuid oibre. Tá tábhacht ar leith ag baint leo seo mar ní hionann cur chuige aon bheirte in ainneoin chomhairle an eagarthóra agus go deimhin, in ainneoin na laincise caoine a choimeád sé orthu. Deirim seo, mar ba chuid den mheitheal mé féin a chuir Béarla ar chúpla dán agus dá réir sin, nach bhfuil neamhchlaon sa ghnó.

Tugann sin go cnag na cúise agus go croí na ceiste sinn – cén dóigh a léifear an leabhar seo agus cad í an chiall a bhainfear as? Is cinnte go léifidh go leor de lucht na hardGhaeilge – iad siúd ar spéis leo an fhilíocht – na dánta sa teanga bhunaidh, ach ba dheacair a shamhlú nach gcaithfeadh siad leathshúil ar a laghad trasna na páirce ar an aistriúchán féachaint conas mar a déanadh an bheart. B'fhéidir gurb í a mhalairt sin a dhéanfaidh léitheoirí Bhéarla a bhfuil smearacháil éigin den Ghaeilge acu, an Béarla a léamh ina uath agus ina aonar mar dhánta iontu féin i dtosach, agus ansin an leathshúil eile a chaitheamh siar d'fhonn tumadh sa bhlaiseadh sin a bhíodh acu nó a bhfuil éileamh acu air. Ní fios do dhuine ar bith a bhfuil seo á léamh aige conas a mheasfar, nó conas a shlogfar sin. Beifear ann, leis, gan amhras, léitheoirí gan focal Gaeilge ar bith a léifidh na leaganacha Béarla mar bhundánta agus gan beann ar bith acu ar na híriglificí ar chlé uathu gur chuma iad nó Araibis nó Incais ina n-aibitrí dúchais. Ba mhór againn a gcuid tuairimí siúd a fháil in am is i dtráth.

Cad is dóigh linne, áfach, atá idir dhá aigne, nó go bhfuil an dá aigne againn? Ní féidir linn géilleadh a choíche ná go deo gurb ionann, ná gurb ar aonchéim é an t-aistriúchán agus an dán féin. Tá ag gach teanga 'its own acoustic sense' mar adeir an t-eagarthóir, agus mar a luann sé mar thagairt do Bhreandán Ó Doibhlin gurb í an Ghaeilge féin 'the only Ariadne's thread guiding us through the fifteen centuries of our recorded history'. Caithfear na macallaí seo a mhaolú is a bhánú is a stoitheadh aníos. Níl aon éalú as sin ach an oiread. Níl dul as ach dul isteach sa bholg, agus níl aon teacht amach as sin. Ní hé go bhfuil aon rud faoi leith míchruinn, óir cad is míchruinneas ann maidir le haistriú fileata de?

Oibríonn a leithéid seo, agus cuireann seo eile thall crithir nimhe trí lár do chnámhdhroma thiar. Leigheas ar bith, níl air sin. Gabhaimis chugainn roinnt samplaí de réir oird isteach:

- Caithfidh go bhfuil 'Tháinig na pianta ar áit na mianta' Uí Dhireáin in 'Ó Mórna' ar cheann de na línte is gliogrúla sa Nua-Ghaeilge, dá bhrí sin, ba chuma cad a dhéanfá leis, feabhas a bheadh ann.

- Ritheann amhrán leis na Police liom nuair a léim 'Every move you make' i gcéad líne 'Ealabhean/Swanwoman', ar nós 'You gave me everything' na Beatles in aistriúchán Frank O'Connor ar 'Caoineadh Airt Uí Laoire', cé nárbh air a bhí an milleán.

- Tá rithim agus go deimhin titim in 'Braithim ag titim an saol' in 'Fiabhras' Uí Ríordáin nach mbeireann 'I feel the world falling apart' air i gceart. Ach i ngach cás mar seo, cad a chuirfeá ina ionad?

- Is maith liom 'to riordanise the glut of unwritten stuff' ar 'Le go ríordánóinn an farasbarr neamhscríte' a bhí fíorghlic ar dtúis.

- Féach seo! 'No escape from her. She/ battens on guts and garters' ar láidre ar shlí é ná a bhfuil i mbundán Mháire Mhac an tSaoi 'Cad is Bean', agus go deimhin tugann éirim bhinbeach íoróineach an dáin sin leis go hiomlán siar síos; agus is cuma cad a dhéanfaidh tú ní féidir ceangal slabhrúil na 'ó-anna' a cheapadh in 'Máiréad sa tsiopa cóirithe gruaige.'

- Bíonn fadhbanna i gcónaí ag leanúint focail nó nathanna a bhféadfadh dhá bhrí a bheith acu. 'Glúin le glúin' Uí Thuairisc in 'Aifreann na Marbh' a bhfuil 'knee to knee' anseo againn. Lá loicht níl air sin, ach gur shíleas riamh go raibh ciall eile sin 'generation' i bhfolach, gan a bheith ródhomhain, sa nath céanna.

- Ansin, laistigh de chúpla líne i ndán gairid 'Hiraeth' Michael Davitt tá 'the day taking a dip in the river' nach bhfuil chomh cumhachtach le 'an lá ag folcadh san abhainn', dar liom, ach dá éis, tá 'glen to glen baying through the cold' ar 'gleann ar ghleann ag tafann tríd an bhfuacht' a bhfuil spionnadh ann nach dtugann 'tafann' leis, dar liom. Nárbh fhearr 'amhastrach' ná 'tafann' ar aon tslí, nó 'sceamhaíl' féin, ach cé mise nó sinne le Davitt a cheartú? Baineann seo ar fad le meáchan agus le blas focal, ar rud pearsanta ar deireadh é sin.

- Cheapas nach bhféadfaí a cheart a thabhairt go deo do línte deiridh sin Davitt in 'Urnaí Maidne', línte a chaitear chugat go neamhthuairimeach ba dhóigh leat, ach a bhfuil pléascán laistiar díobh, ach tá greim ceart orthu anseo: 'Take this cup of tea./ I'm pretty much at death's door./ How about yourself? What's the score?'

- Tá cead tugtha ag Biddy Jenkinson leaganacha próis Bhéarla dá dánta sise a cheadú, agus ní miste a rá go bhfuil siad déanta go cumasach ar an mórchóir, fág rithim agus leagan amach na mbunleaganacha as an áireamh.

Is leor é sin maidir le hiarracht ar mhionghrinneadh a dhéanamh ar chuid de na ceisteanna a phéacann aníos agus a bhfuil ar dhá thaobh na leathanach á bhreithniú. Is maith, leis, gur theorainnigh an t-eagarthóir é féin don 20ú haois, mar tá rabharta agus borradh eile ag teacht aniar ina bhfuil banfhilí go mór chun tosaigh sa chomáint. Smaoinítear go bhfuil nach mór an cúigiú cuid den aois seo cheana caite, agus go bhfuil bóithre móra dúshlánacha le taisteal ag an bhfilíocht seo againn feasta. Ráiteas láidir ealaíonta is ea an leabhar seo ar cheann de ghaiscí liteartha na hÉireann san aois seo caite.

Betty Thompson

PASSING THROUGH

Do you find it dark in the underpass ?
Crab of the thorn, a small light for small people
The travel time is short. I've counted the steps
From start to finish. What's more, St. Lucy
Blesses passers-through, steadies their heartbeat.
Her icon is set into the curvature of the archway.
Look up at the gold leaf glinting. Then emerge
To see the vista of a city farm, its luminous glass
Porch, *eau-de-nil* paling, fronds of faded lavender
On the verge. If you are there, the street is not
Abandoned. On sad days, I try to remember
The name of Johnson's cat, memorialized in bronze
In a London square. It comes eventually, bringing solace.

Note : Line 2 is from 'The Haw Lantern', by Seamus Heaney.

Noel King

KNOWLEDGE FOR ADULTHOOD

> *River water is the last to leave and the first to arrive.*
> *And so times passes. A full life is long.*
> – Leonardo da Vinci

My forefathers were fishermen,
not professional fishermen
but hobby fishermen,
they went to local rivers
Saturdays, Sundays, when their time was off.

Even my grandmother went,
showed us all how to fish,
how to feel a 'pick' on our fingers,
knowing when to give-way, some leeway,
knowing when to jump in and reel in,
knowing when to play the fish, wear him out, tire him
before the final in-for-the-kill landing on the riverbank.
Then the cruel bit, the bashing on the head to kill him,
keeping the lower body unharmed, unstruck,
and later with a carefully chosen knife, slicing him
down his middle, removing the yukky bits.
After that a myriad of cooking ways or freezing for a rainy day.

Both sides of my family fished,
it is said my father asked for my mother's hand in marriage
from her father on the riverbank one Sunday.
I wonder what would have happened if my Granda had refused?

My uncle, my cousins, my nephews all fish,
they are the ones who fish to keep themselves sane,
philosophising in their minds the growing up
of *their* sons and daughters, showing *them* how to fish,
as one goes and one leaves, and so on it goes.

Fiona B Smith

SHELL SHOCK

He built his *laftehus* in the old way,
As it should be done, using cured wood,
Beam on tremendous beam, an X joint
With interlocking notches at the seam.

Sweating over plans, permits, rights of way
Helicopter drops in snow, begging, cajoling
The bureaucrats, architects, authorities.
His wife, to just let him get on with it.

A truffle hog, he sniffed out each stick, churn
Implement, coaxing farmers, dealers,
Collectors to part with their cherished pieces
For him to enshrine in his sacred wooden space.

In the hard work it took to fell trees, drag them,
Haul them across the forest, dig foundations,
And shape the beams, he buried some memories.
Then he nailed a few more into the walls.

You can hear him up there still, pottering, fussing
By the woodpile, stacking tins of condensed milk,
Cod roe from Svolvær, provisions to last him
Until he is forced to cede to a new generation.

Already they come, screwing up his systems,
Logging their jaunts in his cloth-bound cabin book.
The shrieks of their blueberry-trampling children
Irk him as he reads his *National Geographic*.

Alone at night, calm from the cold earth seeps
Up through the well-crafted floorboards,
Contrives to soothe his shell-shocked sleep,
In the one place where he could find peace.

Only the pine marten, the snowy owls, the rut
Of elks to disturb him, at dawn mist clears slowly
As goats file past the stone steps to his door.
Outside, fjord and sky, ready to do his bidding.

Nell Regan

HISTORY LESSONS

Harry Clifton, *Portobello Sonnets* (Bloodaxe Books, 2017), £9.95.
Siobhán Campbell, *Heat Signature* (Seren Books, 2017), £9.99.
Maurice Harmon, *Hoops of Holiness* (Salmon Poetry, 2016), €12.

These three collections were published in the past year but, in varied and intriguing ways, each poet's work speaks from (and then beyond) very specific and different periods in recent Irish history.

In the case of Harry Clifton's *Portobello Sonnets*, this is a particular six-month period in 2004/5, a placing of the self in, among many other things, a pre-crash, newly multicultural Dublin. The collection, which is Harry Clifton's seventh, is an elegantly constructed sonnet cycle that takes place on his return to Dublin, after an absence of sixteen years. The contents page is a found poem in itself, a masterclass in first lines, with 'How to survive the dangerous Dublin stretch', '*(To the singer Freddie White)*', 'Linoleum, yellow light', 'Clouds, too, are incoming information', being just a few examples. The narrator arrives in Dublin's Portobello, in a taxi, 'alive to the danger, in this monkey-puzzle / Of ancestry, this maze of one-way streets'. In 35 regularly rhymed, mostly single stanza sonnets, he begins to explicitly write himself back into Dublin – 'Immerse yourself, disturb the human silt' – and, it transpires, into the third age referenced by the book's epigraph from Patrick Kavanagh, where 'we are content to be ourselves, however small'. The city and the poems are full of identified ghosts, of father, grandfather, and a younger self, as well as of literary forebears, Yeats, Joyce, Beckett, O'Casey, and of course Kavanagh. Early on the narrator exhorts himself to be 'grateful for a day / When nothing happens. Time, pure light / And silence, the world looking the other way.' However, the frustrations of writer's block, its impact on domestic life, and a contemporary literary scene, all impinge.

March brings an uplift, a resolve to 'Sit tight, make little poems, / And stroll the grey canal of an afternoon [...] There are secret sources, / Pure upwellings. Here though, nothing flows, / Least of all water. Peace, the old repose / Of waiting, the daily door that cannot be forced.' Kavanagh's presence is here, but close too is Derek Mahon. The sequence reveals the irony that, in the narrator's letting go of the desire to write 'big' poems, the more lasting work emerges. For this reader that is certainly the case with the subsequent pair of sonnets, the first about a lock-keeper, which is lit like a Dutch painting and opens:

Is there a lockkeeper here, who understands
Slow time, changed levels, endlessly being raised
Beyond ourselves?

And the second which begins:

These are the days that March has lent to April
Under a hard blue dusk of half-lit streets,
A winter retrospective.

Both poems call to mind Emily Dickinson's observation: 'If I feel physically as if the top of my head were taken off, I know *that* is poetry.'

Central to the book is the narrator's discovery of a secular, multicultural Dublin and many of the poems are peopled by North African gentlemen, Chinese altar boys, Lithuanian hairdressers, West Dublin Nigerians, and transmigrating Chinese exes, as well as African, Polish and Mayans using an internet café on Camden Street. At times the tone feels a little uncomfortable (these exotic blow-ins observed by the self-identified latest blow-in, have little interior life), but they are also situated in the context of an 'Emancipated forenoon,' where there is an ...

Ireland drifting away, into a long ago
Policed by myth and terror ...

This beautifully achieved cycle, which yields more and more with every reading, ends at the canal in Rialto, with Christ, Kavanagh, and then Ulysses, who concludes:

To come back from the dead,
Just now, is enough.

Heat Signature is Siobhán Campbell's fourth collection, and its opening poem, 'The shame of our island', marks out some of the varied territory the book will cover, as well as how. It begins with the third last wolf in Ireland, draws the reader in with stark statement, oral history, and hear say, and then swerves to question and address us directly with its last line, 'Is this wolfish?'. Her often chilling last lines don't let anyone off the hook, and this is partly a book about a post-ceasefire, post-crash island:

we have no direction,
rounding again the ring road to the city
as if we knew the story behind the story.

'Framed', ostensibly an amusing yarn of a poem about a Belfast docker with a growth on the back of his neck, also deftly turns on us half-way through with ...

> But there was a reason to begin this ... yes, the
> question of the unborn and the rights of same.

... and we are off, down another path, which concludes with a clergyman called Frame being 'turned' and leaving abruptly to go to 'Somewhere in the outer or the / inner Hebrides they say'.

This acerbic use of oral history, legend, and myth is used to great effect in poems such as 'Uncle Paddy and the man from Atlantis' and 'Interviewing the beast', a muse poem redolent of Nuala Ní Dhomhnaill, by way of Paul Muldoon. The latter's images become an inheritance in the poem 'Periwinkles', when the narrator's northern Irish, Fianna Fáil-canvassing father, shows her around Belfast.

Campbell's formal range and music is evidenced throughout, from the authority of the long line and form of 'Ravens' ('There is a smite of forever in the calluses behind your beak'), and the undercut of the last line 'Here comes the horseman, may I say "pass by"?', to a poem like 'Climb'. The reader is left breathless by its stepped lines and rhyming scheme. Meanwhile the narrator *et al* watch and,

> sip
> our hot chocolate, glancing up
> now and then to make sure
> we're not needed.

The book is punctuated by 'island' poems, and others which directly address both the aftermath of the economic crash and the peace process. While these can be tricky to pull off, they all have some feature that is memorable and sharp. The narrator satirises and punctures the often self-serving myths of 'the island' ('Hell is an island of too many horizons').

Campbell is concerned with the act of seeing, in all its various forms and tones. So, in the sonnet 'Camouflage', when a child 'out collecting rubber bullets' for pocket money, encounters soldiers, 'Watching is too small a word.' In 'Concentration', a poem about her grandmother, she concludes that:

> When things attract our deep attention
> they give back out the stare that we put in ...

And then there is the delight, in 'Weeding', of:

> seeing things anew, filthy
> with possibility ...

These ways of seeing are part of the poetic impulse in Campbell's work, but there is a second pressing imperative which is found in the last line of the book, ostensibly about morels: 'If we do not gather them, who will?'

'I belong to open spaces' is the cry of the main character in Maurice Harmon's libretto, 'Tales Out of School', as he enters a seminary in his early teens. There he meets the 'taut / bare faces' of his fellows and suffers a loss of innocence, as well as meeting the brutality and hypocrisy of mid-twentieth century Irish Catholicism. It creates such a distance between him and his former life that he cannot fit in on his return home; he is 'A white blackbird', and 'A misfit in my own place.' His parents lament that,

> When the years go,
> They cannot be brought back.
> When the plane eases the wood
> It takes a new shape.

The libretto, written for a two-act opera *The Chosen Few* by Derek Ball, forms about a quarter of Maurice Harmon's sixth collection, *Hoops of Holiness*. Love of the outdoors and the horrors wrought by this particular form of Catholic dogma also drive and inform much of the rest of the book. The narrator's anger and despair at the sexual distortion and cruelties inflicted by the Church is palpable. The abrupt end of that power is captured in the title poem, 'Hoops of Holiness'. Here 'an entire people shuffling to the big door, / hearing about a man-god thorned, / a stone rolled back', where 'All that mattered was the appearance of belief.' The priest in the poem, who 'held his peace/ when he should have held his ground', is 'Like a horse turned out to grass'; there are echoes here of Kavanagh's 'The Great Hunger'.

There are also lighter poems in the collection, relayed in Harmon's mischievous and affectionate tone. The opening poem, 'Man in a Straw Hat', has the narrator in his 'old duds' relishing the sight and sounds of birds about their business, while another concerns the shameless antics of pigeons in love; there is also the narrator slipping out of a poetry reading and on a visit to the doctor, with the opening line: 'When I visit Balor on the hill he rolls one eye'.

For this reader, the work is more convincing when it is powered by fresh images and form rather than exposition, as this allows us inside. The poem 'Camping' ends with:

I am nowhere to be seen

I sit here
Remembering
A bead of ink
Listening

Elsewhere, in 'Flight', one brave soul tries to escape school and despite his failure, has 'the seat by the fire / whose heat the rest of us no longer felt'.

Occasionally the reader stumbles over the use of or absence of pronouns, and it's unclear which character is being referred to – this is particularly tricky in the poem 'Fr. Socius', as it seems to deal with clerical abuse. However, there are moving elegies here too, including the first section of 'Woman in Black', previously published as 'Dún Dealgan', and 'In the Green', for Dennis O'Driscoll. The poetry section of the book ends with the acceptance and 'open space' of the poem, 'A Strange Shore':

It is beautiful
All of a piece
We do not speak

As we turn she goes left
I walk back alone
on a strange shore

Michael Brophy

BORDER LINES

An infant's cheek rests on the warmth
Of her knee, his head pressed against
The crocodile skin of her handbag

As she gently strokes his hair while
The Enterprise smokes its way home
With her Christmas catch of cologne.

Altar boys on their annual outing
Punching the air as letterboxes
Change from red to green

Excited to visit once more the glass
Displays of elderly weapons and the
Slouched hats of mannequin soldiers.

Students driving north coughing on
Full-strength roll-ups to smother the smell
Of plastic packages inside the doors.

A son crossing south with his father's
Urn hidden in a towel to release
Him without formal approval for
Resting in peace.

Gerard Fanning

FOR THE LOVE OF HOPS

Tip-toeing on our new fence, put up in a few hours
by two Wexford men who barely spoke a word,

he parries with feint and riposte for the nuts
and black suet ball which we comically offer

as our offhand gesture to unravel the food chain.
And make no mistake, his bustle curled and flexed

has as much to do with balance as applause.
Boxing clever, this southpaw of a thought too far

may sup from our cup, but should the fence
succumb to rot for lack of a spit of creosote,

or the flaking gazebo shift ground in a thaw,
or his very own sense of self, mitts at the ready,

lean to feral out of boredom, tired of being
offered saucers of leftovers, then as often

as he steadies to go back to his stand
of Holm oaks, he returns for one more snifter,

the lure of hops perhaps greater, in the upturned
optic of the birdfeeder's dispenser.

Gráinne Tobin

INTER-RAIL

The tired boy sharing her seat looked into her eyes
the day they took him off the Budapest train.

Now wood pigeons coocoo in the hotel garden
as a lizard traverses a wall and makes no noise,
and in the time it takes for nail polish to dry,
some day is saved, some life is lost.

She reads a magazine whose cover promises
to ask celebrities how one can be happy,
with a piece inside that says, when fish stocks fail,
seagulls develop a taste for landfill and trash,
and an exquisite photo of psychedelic sewage,
marbling a canal in swirls of purple and green.

She visits megaliths which echo for two hands clapping,
as hummingbird hawk moths flicker in the hedge,
and she washes her hands, unobserved, in the font
of a church in a foreign street, by a mural
of Germaine Tillion, home from Ravensbrück,
who kept a good table for guests and lived to a hundred.

Barbed wire enclosures are under construction
beside railway lines on several borders.

She will think of that boy as long as she lives.
How will her own house be remembered?

Susan Kelly

THE BITTERSWEET

Her passion was historical biscuit tins,
or so he'd tell visitors
who marvelled at the growing stacks of embossed lids
that glinted with landscapes, landmarks,
locations she hadn't seen,
he thought it best if the world came to her.
He liked her to display these gifts he brought back
from places he visited with work.
Work, that was what he called her.

He'd produce a new one
the morning after his return,
assuming her quietness over breakfast
was due to the non-presentation of a tin.
She accepted them,
but never the treats
that she bagged in black
where they grew crumbly and green
and sweated in the confines of their own wrappings.

No tins came for some months,
work no longer needed him
so he dozed his days away in front of the box
until he breathed his last,
the remote control limp in his hand.
She scattered the tins around the living room
and took a hammer to the shiny lids
that remembered everywhere she had never been,
until they didn't shine anymore.

Dandelion / Taraxacum officinale by **Yanny Petters**
Verre Églomisé / painting on glass, 42 cm x 33 cm
www.yannypetters.net

All of the images in this issue are from artists represented by the Olivier Cornet Gallery, 3 Great Denmark Street (off Parnell Square), Dublin 1 (**www.oliviercornetgallery.com**)

Emptiness exists in the form of a Top Hat by Brad Gray
Oil on Canvas, 46 cm x 50 cm
www.bradgrayartist.com

Stained silver spoon by Miriam McConnon
Oil on canvas, 25 cm x 25 cm
www.miriammcconnonart.com

Brown-eyed girl by Eoin Mac Lochlainn
Oil on canvas, 80 cm x 90 cm
www.eoinmaclochlainn.com

Citadel III – Ecuadorian Embassy by Claire Halpin
Oil on Gesso, 37 cm x 57 cm
https://clairehalpin2011.wordpress.com

Dressed for Success by **Kelly Ratchford**
Acrylic, ink and charcoal on wood panel, 12 cm x 8 cm
www.kellyratchford.com

Seán Lysaght

ATHENA

In which he recognises her wisdom,
but is unable to receive it until he stops desiring her.

A swirl of dust on a curving track,
A gritty cloud, bringing Athena,
Sets her down like an insolent girl
In a magazine ad, too proud to say
Why she's there.

I let her strike the pose, then add
Voice-over, the first words mine:

"Regina, there's trouble in the kingdom,
The coast is covered with the slough they cast
When they hatched like mayflies in their thousands.
They slit the bellies of their boats and went inland,
With everything forbidden, except the walk to find you."

And then these words from her:

"You think this small trace of the present
Is enough to conjure me? I know
You saw a photograph of a traveller girl
And thought you would strike my image there.
Only in her remoteness
You supposed you could overcome desire."

"Regina, I – "

"There isn't a princess for everyone,
That's why I make them work.
And you hedged my image with the owl,
You waited after twilight for a call
That would redeem the cold of your country.
Now you make me smile with the pathos
Of your defeated wish, and still you think
To win me. Even this sympathy
Has you written all over it."

Athena's speech had lit her absent face.
I stepped forward, to know more,
But a wind rose, and it claimed her
With another blinding dust.
When my eyes could look again,
There was just an empty arc of road
Stretching away –
                                        and a memory of her smile,
The one thing antiquity could not spirit back.

Liam Harrison

DISTANT SCREAMS FROM THE BRIDGE: DEREK MAHON AND EDVARD MUNCH

> Grave daughters
> of time, you lightly toss
> your hair as the long shadows grow
> and night begins to fall.
> – 'Girls on the Bridge', Derek Mahon

Derek Mahon's poems are concerned with apocalyptic transitions, those critical, age-defining moments of terror which strike at the heart of humanity. Yet instead of focusing on pivotal historic twists, or on the hell-fire raining down, Mahon's poetry looks to the margins, delving into the everyday perseverance of lives after tragedies, lives which are haunted in a post-traumatic world. In Mahon's most famous poem, 'A Disused Shed in Co Wexford', we hear 'only the ghost of a scream' from the voiceless victims of atrocities ('Treblinka and Pompeii') who silently implore us to 'speak on their behalf'.

The echoes of these atrocities can feel endless, as the themes across Mahon's poetry span holocausts, ecological disasters, terrorism, wars, and famines. At times it seems as if the poetic voices are speaking from a point of 'late history' – speaking with a note of terminal pathos, giving the sense of being resigned to the fates they have received, or resigned to the fates to come. As the ambivalent, perhaps ironically titled 'Everything is Going to be All Right' dismissively states, 'There will be dying, there will be dying, / but there is no need to go into that'. It is as though we are nearing the close of Stephen Dedalus's historical nightmare, or hearing posthumous murmurs long after Francis Fukuyama's 'end of history'.

Yet Mahon's poetry also manages to reverse this late historical quality, by minutely focusing on those simmering moments just before disaster strikes; the dark clouds are gathering before the storm, and we are casually sipping drinks in Pompeii, stepping aboard the Titanic, securing 'peace for our time' in Munich, about to start our rigged car in Belfast. The poetic voice anticipates the ghosts to come.

One of Mahon's many poignant gifts is his ability to turn the apocalyptic fervour of the world at large (that sense of global dread many currently experience when surveying the daily headlines), and localise it in a transient, everyday setting. The heights scaled by Mahon's lyrics are matched by the images he conjures in these ordinary scenes. This is especially true in his ekphrastic poetry, which display a captivating, beguiling attention to sound and light when passing over seemingly commonplace moments. These poems of sound and vision are capable of reducing the catastrophes of the world to an evening walk at sunset, or amplifying a single scream into the death-cry for all mankind.

The poem 'Girls on the Bridge', originally published in the 1982 collection *The Hunt by Night*, encapsulates this sensation of a quotidian apocalypse. It shifts hazily between two Edvard Munch paintings – from the peaceful 'The Girls on the Pier' (1900) to the famous 'The Scream' (1893). The poem starts during the golden hour of evening in the former painting, with the girls full of 'adolescent hopes / and privileges', staying out late on a bridge in Åsgårdstrand, gossiping with their 'quiet conversational quack / expressive of calm days / and peace of mind'. But in the final stanzas the light starts to dim, 'night begins to fall', and the world fades from one of optimistic wonder to the twilit vertigo of the Munchian Scream:

> a ghastly sun
> watches in pale dismay.
> Oh you may laugh, being as you are
> fair sisters of the evening star,
> but wait – if not today
> a day will dawn
>
> when the bad dreams
> you scarcely know will scatter
> the punctual increment of your lives.
> The road resumes, and where it curves,
> a mile from where you chatter,
> somebody screams.

The earlier moments of youth and innocence on the riverbanks, where the girls listlessly gazed upon the 'unplumbed, reflective lake', are starkly contrasted against the impending screams of history. Merely a mile away there is a looming nightmare from which the privileged girls will be unable to wake. Terence Brown has pointedly remarked how the poem's initial setting of ('Beds, / lamplight and crisp linen') resonates more closely with Dutch Golden Age paintings of domesticity rather than the *fin-de-siècle* angst which Munch's works are typically known for. This rare escape from the anxiety of Munch's world, however, only serves to intensify the scream when it comes; the moment of serenity only emphasising the impending horrors.

After reading the poem through to its eerie conclusion, it is impossible to revisit the earlier peaceful scenes without a perverse knowledge of the deathly future to come. The girls' 'sedate / limbs and averted heads' now assume an uncanny air, severed from their present lives. Rereading disturbs the temporality of the poem, as now the idyllic pre-apocalyptic scene is contaminated by a sense of anachronism, bound up in our anticipation. This quality is prevalent across Mahon's poetry, where the present position of the speaker (and reader) often feels undercut, as if the poem is speaking from a distinct point 'before the scream', or 'after the tragedy'. The latter sensation features prominently in Mahon's poem 'After the Titanic', which considers the high-ranking official J Bruce Ismay who survived the sinking, 'Then it is / I drown again with all those dim / Lost faces'. These lucid moments, frequently captured across Mahon's poetry, are cast in a sharp pre-traumatic or post-traumatic light.

Mahon is famous (or infamous) for revising his poetry, a habit which further shifts the ground upon which the poems are constructed. In his review for the *Dublin Review of Books* of the most recent *New Collected Poems* (2016), David Wheatley starts by counting the casualties of the latest collection, lamenting those discarded lines and severed stanzas. 'Girls on the Bridge' has similarly been edited and re-edited. Mahon had previously written additional stanzas which complete the deathly trajectory of the poem after the scream. They begin, 'The girls are dead / The house and pond are gone'. But these lines were cut in later versions of the poem to maintain the sense of sinister ambiguity, and to keep the girls and reader precisely caught up in the moment of uncertainty. The extended version of the poem, with its blunt confirmation of death, clearly diminishes the anticipatory angst and dread of the future which the final note of the distant scream conjures so successfully in the shorter version.

Wheatley similarly notes that if the cries for help from the victims in 'A Disused Shed in Co Wexford' were answered in the poem, the sense of resolution would render the scene sanitised and banal. It is the artistic pose of being 'caught in the moment, arraigned by history and unsure how to proceed' which Wheatley values in Mahon's poetry. Likewise, in Mahon's poem 'Leaves', it is again the sense of anticipation, of vague afterlives and lost futures, which gives the poem its dramatic resonance: 'Somewhere there is an afterlife / of dead leaves'. Like the scream in 'Girls on the Bridge', the sense of distance, the displacement of 'somewhere', maintains the unnerving ambiguity of the poetic balance.

'Leaves' ends by dwelling on the alternative paths the reader, poet, and poem may have taken, 'the lives we might have led / have found their own fulfilment'. The anticipation and aporia which are perfectly posed in the poem feed into Mahon's own pattern of writing and rewriting his work. This pattern further distorts any attempts to read the poems in a neatly linear fashion. Deaths are erased, futures are displaced, and inflections are altered, to the extent that we are wary when reading and rereading Mahon that we may not ever be crossing the same path again. Mahon's 'Heraclitus on Rivers' says as much – 'Nobody steps into the same river twice'.

Questions of time and linearity also emerge in Mahon's brief epigram to 'Girls on the Bridge' – 'Munch 1901' – directing the reader to the dating of the painting (an inaccurate dating, some have argued, as Munch painted several similar paintings with the same bridge motif). The year is the beginning of that low, dishonest century, which perhaps alludes to the forthcoming 'bad dreams' of war, death and destruction which will soon disturb so many incremental, ordinary lives. It was on an evening walk towards the turn of the previous century that Munch found inspiration for 'The Scream'. His personal account resonates with the tremulous finale of the poem:

> I was walking along the road with two friends – the sun was setting – suddenly the sky turned blood red – I paused, feeling exhausted, and leaned on the fence – there was blood and tongues of fire above the blue-black fjord and the city – my friends walked on, and I stood there trembling with anxiety – and I sensed an infinite scream passing through nature.

We are subject to the 'ghastly sun' from Munch's painting and Mahon's poem, unleashing its hellish tongues of fire over the sky, with Munch himself caught in an inferno of anxiety. Although the painting is popularly called 'The Scream', perhaps indicating an individual shriek, Munch actually called the painting 'Der Schrei der Natur' or 'The Scream of Nature'. This full title can be seen to transpose the painting, in a similar manner to Mahon's poem, from an individual scream into an 'infinite scream' for all nature, all humanity. Another poem of Mahon's, 'Autumn Skies', also expresses the transition Munch captures, of the particular fading into the universal: 'If a thing happens once / it happens once for ever'.

In what may initially sound like the opposite of the Munchian scream, Terence Brown has claimed that 'austere nostalgia' is one of the quintessential notes in Mahon's poetry. It is a phrase which unravels to convey Mahon's own fascination with the visual arts – the 'austere' stillness of the reflective image, the numinous quality of painting, as well as the protean and ceaseless capacities of nostalgia and memory. As Brown puts it:

> Mahon responds with such reverence to moments like that recorded in Munch's painting ['The Girls on the Pier'], when the world achieves a momentary, significant stasis, because his own imagination is profoundly attracted to such epiphanic, luminous occasions in life itself.

Yet it can also be argued that Mahon is simultaneously drawn to the fragmented qualities of these epiphanic moments as well. Even as it is captured, the 'significant stasis' of the image is unsettled in 'Girls on the Bridge' by the blurring of separate artworks and art forms – the stillness is pierced by the echoes of the quivering scream. The relationship between painting and poem in 'Girls on the Bridge' serves to disturb the idea of one unified image. Even as the two mediums fixate on the one still scene of girls dawdling on a bridge, the differing modes of art create a friction, a friction which points to a fundamental anxiety in the act of representation. The distrust of representational, mimetic art can be seen as Mahon's literary inheritance from Samuel Beckett, playing on the dual artistic obligation to express and the impossibility to do so. In this post-Beckett vein, the words depicting the peaceful girls can begin to seem slippery, deceitful, and the image, once still, is now trembling, reverberating with terror. The closing scream of the poem adds another dimension to the image, perforating the stability of the initial scene, and performing a kind of anti-epiphany, representing the vague, distant and unknown fears soon to encroach upon the girls' lives, and upon the lives of many others.

The multi-layering of different artworks and forms plays into Mahon's aesthetic as a highly allusive poet, often writing poems 'after' other artists and artworks. Tom Walker similarly notes that Mahon's poems give voice to 'the aftermath of overt kinds of transgression'. By giving voice to the post-traumatic aftermath of events, or anxiously 'pre-traumatically' anticipating these events, we can again see how Mahon's poems are often haunted by a post-ness, a sense of lateness. This allusive anxiety is at the heart of ekphrastic poetry, which as the 'verbal representation of visual representation' transgresses aesthetic borders, creating something markedly different from a singularly written or visual form. The new forms contain a posthumous, ghostly imprint of the original, whilst transforming those old images and forms into something rich and strange.

Throughout Mahon's poetry the words and images appear to be undergoing a constant sea change, an apocalyptic turning (and turning). In 'Girls on the Bridge', what at first appeared to be two forms of the same still image – girls lingering on a bridge – shifts into a liminal aesthetic space, to be crossed many times over. We keep oscillating between image and words, from the paintings of tranquil bridge to screaming bridge, from the immediacy of the present to the horrors of history, from personal experience to universal suffering – never fixing still on one in particular. The screams in the distance puncture our everyday lives, whilst we cannot discern if they are the screams of the past, or terrors, just around the curved road, to come.

References
Terence Brown: www.jstor.org/stable/25484593?seq=1#page_scan_tab_contents
David Wheatley: www.drb.ie/essays/picking-at-it
Tom Walker: www.tcd.ie/trinitywriters/writers/derek-mahon

Michael McCarthy

THE JACKET

I still don't know what came between us.
We had been great with each other for years.
I was a mentor when you were growing up.
I watched with pride as you spread your wings.
I didn't believe it at first, the snubs, the bad vibes,
I thought I must be imagining things. Soon enough
it became all too clear that everything had gone sour.

The jacket of Donegal Tweed was a thank you gift
for my small mercies. I reserved it for big occasions,
Grand National Day or the Cheltenham Gold Cup.
I loved the velvety insides, the rough texture of the lapels.
It was the one thing I thought might survive our demise.
But when I tried it on after your final *coup de grâce*
the chill of you had insinuated itself in the sleeves.

Years later we patched things up, though we never
got to the bottom of what it was caused the rupture.
I had kept the jacket as a reminder of our past, thinking:
we'll always have Paris, even if everything else was lost.
I never wore it again. The feelings were way too raw.
But I held on to it, wrapped in polythene at the back
of the wardrobe, as I moved on from place to place.

Things levelled out, we were civil whenever we met.
At certain moments some of the old warmth came back.
We've been fine for years now, all that stuff in the past.
I came across the jacket last week on an annual clear-out.
The speckled green is pristine, the lining smooth and cool.
the elbow patches and leather buttons rugged and strong,
and it still fits. But the shiver of your stare has clung on.

Clodagh Beresford Dunne

THE RADIOGRAPHER

Hear the buzzhum to catch those ghostly shadows

Like a perfume plume
you arrived in the world one Bloomsday –
a button-nosed blonde with a mind of her own.

You slept in a bed for a crib
drank Coca-Cola not infant milk
had a candour at three that was unparalleled

broke news of death with a jolt of coldness
opened doors to poets in Decembers
with *Too late! They're dead!*

You ate your meals with a mermaid's dingo hopper
watched horrors each night before bed
attuned yourself to the earth's core

listened for each murmur, focused on each movement.
Your acuteness
lived up to every meaning of your name

Katie: frank and scientific.
You netted each prize throughout school
engineered a loop road to ease congestion

created flow in one direction
found the radix of each problem
like Röntgen, produced, detected and saw through.

Piotr Florczyk

LIEU DE MÉMOIRE

Two trains leave the station
at the same time, blowing their whistles
unceremoniously.

Heading east the one with five cars
travels 20 miles per hour
faster than the other, which is also
heading east.

Both trains will reach their destination
after two hundred miles.

What is the speed of the train
with ten cars, and why
does it eventually return
empty?

Martina Dalton

LILAC

Its colour
ground from mountains.

Its waxy stars, soft,
the in-between colour
of a newborn's eyes.

Hides its rust
on its underside,
ashamed
it paid too close attention
to Autumn's turn.

Snipped
it has the weight
of a deflating balloon.

Drop it
and it makes no sound.

Breda Wall Ryan

NATURAL SELECTION

Noel Monahan, *Where the Wind Sleeps: New and Selected Poems* (Salmon Poetry, 2014), €14.
Jean O'Brien, *Fish on a Bicycle: New and Selected Poems* (Salmon Poetry, 2016), €14.

Noel Monahan's *Where the Wind Sleeps* begins with his recent work, then samples five previous collections in reverse chronology through to his debut, *Opposite Walls*. Throughout, he has brought his everyday surroundings under the microscope, bringing subtle social changes into sharp focus, highlighting a significance that might otherwise be missed.

> Remember the convent?
> It's a restaurant now.
> The few remaining nuns
> Renamed themselves
> And left for a bungalow on the hill.
> – 'THE OLDE PRIORY' (1991)

His language and imagery are coloured by the rhythms and cadences of the Irish language in which he also writes. The delightful 'Bealtaine' / 'The Month of May' and 'Ciaróg Dubh' / 'Cockroach', both from *Curve of the Moon* (2010), are presented here in dual text format. Monahan has also taken up the challenge of re-imagining, for a modern readership and audience, the anti-hero of the Irish medieval legend *Buile Suibhne*. His *Suibhne Faoi Bhodhrán Ghealaí / Sweeney Under A Full Moon*, written in modern Irish and translated by the poet, follows Sweeney's punitive sojourn as bird-man in The-In-Between, until his eventual redemption:

> Ag eitilt is ag síor eitilt
> Ó sceach geal go sceach thalún
> Feothan gaoithe ina aghaidh
> [...]
> Sceach ina scórnach ...
>
> Forever flying about the place
> From whitethorn to briar
> Gust of wind in his face
> [...]
> A crow in the throat ...

Written for voice and choral music, the poem has a strong aural component and rewards reading aloud.

'We are an inward-looking people', the tour-guide says in 'Marrakech'. Monahan might well be defining his poetic vision with those words. The selection presented here explores the In-Between where myth and the real world share a landscape, where the poet delves deep to bring us his reflections on time and place and the human condition. His homage to Swift in the gently satirical 'A Ghostly Letter from Sheridan to Swift', ends its acerbic observations with a harsh conclusion, cloaked in humour:

> On second thoughts, not much has changed,
> It's just a little more deranged,
> [...]
> *"The Legion Club"*, open to bribe,
> Is now *"The Dáil"*, curse of the tribe.

In the final poem from *Curve Of The Moon*, the nostalgically charming 'December Extract from Diary of a Town', Monahan employs his skills as both dramatist and poet. He records the minutiae of a rural community with affection, invents evocative nicknames for his protagonists – Busty Maherty, The Danger Smith – and lists the exotic ingredients purchased for Christmas cake. This contrasts with 'Granada Ballroom' and 'Scar on a Country Town' (from *Opposite Walls*, 1991), where the poet's forensic gaze on parochial mores is softened by compassion.

Like Kavanagh, whom he celebrates in his sonnet 'Beyond the Wind', Monahan is a poet whose observations and language are steeped in nature. His description, from 'The Calf-Bearer' ...

> He knows the agony of clay, the language
> Of weather, blaze of the sun, squally winds,
> Apples dropping on the lap of autumn,
> Winter under the trees of the moon.

... could equally apply to his own poetry, especially in the section titled *Drumlins*, a series of carefully crafted sonnets, many rooted in Ireland's Christian tradition but aware of the contemporary post-Christian reality. Irish and foreign place names, saints' names, ruined monasteries, figures from Greek mythology, Frida Kahlo's white dress, the cry of the Banshee, all have their place in creating an ambience of lonely quest. The sonnets, complete in themselves, reward dipping into at random, but perhaps there is a greater reward to be had by reading the entire sequence for its unity, which reflects the poet's search for his, and humankind's, place on the earth and in the In-Between-Realm of thoughtful introspection. Whether begun at the beginning with the new poems, or at the end, in order to accompany the poet on his journey, *Where the Wind Sleeps* is an engrossing collection, where, 'you can eavesdrop on the wind / And listen to the procession of years / Go past'.

Fish on a Bicycle, the title of Jean O'Brien's *New and Selected Poems*, together with its cover image based on a Kevin McSherry print, capture the essence of her poetic aesthetic, identifying her unambiguously to new readers as an assured and skillful lyric poet. A quick browse through the selection here reveals an honest and thoughtful preoccupation with loss of all kinds, a theme which runs through all her collections since her first chapbook, *Working the Flow* (Lapwing Publications, 1992). Here, in the opening poem, 'The Dreaming', perhaps the poet's *Ars Poetica* in the guise of an origins story, we learn: 'the hot sand like pumice / strips off the grace notes / while my skin shifts to encompass / the loss'.

Loss of other kinds follows. The female mountaineer in 'Everest' has lost her life in her attempt on the mountain. The language used here is tender, filled with compassion:

> the elements are slowly undressing her,
> she is being stripped off as the mountain
> sculpts itself around her, folding her in.

Nobody, the poem implies, conquers death. The poet looks it in the eye, unblinking, accepting: 'crevasses yawn before us. Then, as if reaching / for the heavens, we climb on'. The theme of death recurs throughout *Fish on a Bicycle*, the poet returning to it, and more specifically – at regular intervals – returning to the death of her mother. 'Learning Death', written in the third person, traces a child's first encounter with death; a dead fly and her mother's explanation:

> the silent – still – black – nothingness.
> The no more of it.
> [...]
> she wondered if her mother
> had been teaching her
> her own death.

A few pages further, in 'Wheeling down the Towpath', the mother is a vivid, haunting childhood memory which the speaker relives before concluding that it may be time to put such memories aside:

> ...the image
> of your receding shape is locked
> in my mind.
> [...]

I wait now for the sign
that will tell me to stop following
and finally let you go.

Other deaths find their way into O'Brien's poems. In 'A Body Recovered', O'Brien's matter-of-fact tone derives from colloquial reportage, before lifting into the realm of lyric in the closing lines: 'That night as I built the fire up / with brown turf. The flame rose / like a fanfare.' There are other elegies, too: 'On Shellinghill Beach' is a first-person exploration of the torture and murder of Jean McConville; 'Memory Wintering (*for Sheila*)' mourns a mind lost to dementia.

Yet *Fish on a Bicycle* is not in any way a difficult read; the poems that treat of death are for the most part lightly handled, and all the more effective for being so. The collection is arranged so that the 'darker' poems are interspersed among other mother-themed poems which capture happier memories: 'The Recipe', 'Her Old Black Bike', the joyful 'The Arc of the Swing' and 'Sound Waves', among others. There is joy and humour in 'Letter to my Darling Daughter, and in 'Rebel, Rebel':

In the turn of my daughter's slender wrist I see it,
the title of a Bowie song from the seventies.

'Hatching the Vision', in which an impatient teenager is preparing to shrug off parental supervision, is filled with a delightful combination of exuberance and exasperation: 'no moss will gather, she is on the move, / a stone rolling. [...] *I'm outta here.*' 'Uncharted Lanes' captures unfettered summer days when children roamed at will in a time when 'unstructured play' was the norm.

O'Brien's new poems, presented here at the end of the collection, are more contemplative. The longer lines allow the reader to 'listen in' to the poet's thinking process. They also suit her narrative style, particularly the first person narration of the award-winning 'Merman', which employs mythology to explore sexual harassment and rape in the workplace.

In 'The Mirror Demons' we read:

All I do is take in the light
  that hits me and bounce it back.

But O'Brien does more than that; she goes deep under the surface of things. *Fish on a Bicycle* contains some of her finest work and deserves close reading not only for its mirror-smooth surface, but also for its concealed depths.

Cathal Ó Searcaigh

AG GUÍ CHUN NA GEALAÍ

Siúd ag éirí í in iomlán a glóire,
uasal, álainn, ríogúil;
siúd ag éirí í, gealach an tsamhraidh,
as leabaidh gheal na néal
le gabháil i mbun a dualgaisí,
a cúramaí mórthaibhseacha oíche.
Bandia an tSolais! Sorcha Mhór na Glóire!
Siúd í ag tabhairt a haghaidhe
agus lí a háilleachta ar na críocha dorcha.
Agus mar is dual do lucht na hÉigse,
seo mé ar mo ghlúine ag umhlú daoithi.
Lasair na díograise! Laom na tuigse!
Iarraim uirthi anois léas solais
a thabhairt do na daoine uaigneacha
atá ag siúl na hoíche
ag cuartú cuideachta.
Iarraim uirthi sleamhnú faoi rún
isteach i bpríosún; a port binn sóláis
a chanadh i gcampaí géibhinn;
a bheith ina réalt' eolais
ag teifigh atá ag éalú thar toinn;
a cuid eochracha óir, na cinn
is fóirsteanaí ina stór
a shíneadh chuig na hoibrithe
atá faoi ghlas agus i sáinn
i dtithe striapaigh, i bpoill mhianaigh, in allaslainn.
Iarraim uirthi cuairt reatha
a thabhairt ar otharlainn
ag beannú do theacht agus d'imeacht na beatha.
Iarraim uirthi a cogar rúin
a chur i gcluasa na leannán,
á ngríosadh sa dóigh nach mbíonn siad
faoi chuing na cúthaileachta
agus iad ag déanamh cumainn.
Iarraim uirthi méar chaoin
an tsóláis a leagan ar éadan
an té atá breoite i gcolainn
nó atá buartha san intinn.
Iarraim uirthi a bheith ceansa

leis na geilt a théann le gealaí
nuair a tchí siad ansiúd í
in iomlán nocht a glóire.
Iarraim uirthi iad a chur ar shlí
a leasa óir is í a mheallann chuici iad
faoi gheasa diamhra a cumhachta.
Iarraim uirthi, géagálainn na gluaiseachta,
í féin a thaispeáint ar bhlár an áir
in Aleppo, i mBaghdad, i San'aa,
agus ní mar bhlaosc lom an bháis
ach mar ghnúis bheo na daonnachta.
Anois agus í i mbarr a réime
ag féachaint anuas orainn go báúil,
iarraim a beannacht agus a coimirce go lá,
ar a bhfuil beo agus ag beathú
ar an domhan bocht suaite seo
atá lán de ghleo agus de chrá.
Iarraim a beannacht anocht.
Tá gá againn uilig le gaethe a Grá.

Cathal Ó Searcaigh

SA SOUK

Idir stainnín na mban
agus seastán na gcumhrán
bhuail mé le haingeal;
an sciathán a bhí síos leis
deasaithe i mbindealán bán.
Chan gan saothar ba léir
a thuirling sé ar an tsaol.
D'fhéach sé orm go géar
ag cur in iúl domh go sochmaidh
go raibh cumann eadrainn seal
i bhfad ó shoin sa Bhaibealóin,
gaol nach dtáinig chun cinn, faraor,
de bharr saol na linne,
ach anois bhí linn ...

                                        D'fhéach sé orm,
a ghnúis ainglí lasta le díograis.
Bhí fonn air, a dúirt sé, ár gcumann,
ár ngrá éagmaise ón tseanré
a thabhairt chun solais.
Faraor, bhí mo sháith os mo choinnese
an saol seo, a dúirt mé leis,
a thabhairt chun léire is grinnis
gan trácht ar an tsaol úd
a bhí curtha i gcré na Baibealóine.
Lena chois sin bhí am tae ann
rud a ba phráinní i bhfad
ná a bheith ag tochailt sa tseanré.

Idir stainnín na mban
agus seastán na gcumhrán
d'fhág mé slán
ag m'aingeal beag geal
agus é ar leathsciathán
ach bhí fhios agam
nach mbeadh ann ach seal
go dtuirlingeodh sé
ar dhuine éigin eile lena dhea-scéala.
Is cinnte go raibh siad ann
a chuirfeadh fáilte roimh aingeal.

Gerard Coughlan

DERNIER

Towards the end of its cycle
Our dishwasher idles,
Emitting a soft, soporific sound.

I am forever put in mind
Of the Dublin to Cork train,
Beginning its slow descent
To Kent Station
On a winter's evening –

Bringing, in its wake,
A cloak of darkening countryside:
Raven-possessed oaks,
Yellow-eyed windows
Of brave, misted bungalows
And silvered water, in lonely fields,
Catching the vanity
Of an aloof and
Always indifferent moon.

Eriko Tsugawa-Madden

SEAGULLS

Two seagulls on the chimney mew.
The sea, not far away but not so close either.
Why they come here I don't know.

They don't see much from the chimney,
only some trees, the hills in the distance
and sparse, tired looking pedestrians.

Here offers nothing you could eat.
You want herring eyes, don't you?

Two seagulls on the roof top mew.
Robins and tits who hear their cry
hide in the thick bush.

Declan Sweeney

ANCESTRY

One day someone from America
will arrive in the village with
your name on a piece of paper and a map
of the graveyard. He might have one of those
faded photographs, recently discovered on a neglected spool
– all those young men in white shirts
beneath the tree in Cahill's garden the tree he will identify; still standing
but no one knows the young girl that made you look happy. All
the boys have passed, as they say. This
distant relative searching for his roots will not have
observed you in the flesh, as I have, circling
the square, in such a way that made it an act of
remembering. I can only imagine what you were trying to remember
but it looked important, like a man knowing he had little time, like
that moment I stood in the doorway and watched you, unguarded
sitting on the side of the bed and staring out at the trees.
This man will seek you out as I never have
but he will never see the way you opened and closed your hands
when you felt overwhelmed by mystery.

RICHARD MURPHY IN SRI LANKA: AN INTERVIEW

On a visit to Sri Lanka in January 2015, **Ben Keatinge** had the opportunity to discuss with **Richard Murphy** his long association with Sri Lanka / Ceylon in both his early childhood and later life. The discussion took place in The Octagon, a building designed by Richard Murphy beside his home on a former tea estate near Kandy, Central Province, Sri Lanka, where he has lived in retirement since 2007.

BK: Can you tell us a little about your early memories of growing up as a child in Sri Lanka?

RM: It was a Crown colony of the British Empire in those days. My father, who was born in a rectory in Ballinlough, Co Roscommon, studied classics at Tipperary Grammar School and Trinity College, Dublin, and from 1910 spent 32 years in the Ceylon Civil Service. I spent five of my early childhood years in this country, and one of the happiest memories I had, and my sisters and brothers also had, was of our holidays in the hills which are cooler than the sea coast. But we lived in Colombo most of the time. And in 1933 when I was six years old, I and my older brother and older sister and parents witnessed the great *Perahera* from the Temple of the Sacred Tooth of the Buddha in Kandy, from the Temple balcony itself. It was an enormous privilege to be invited by the chief monk of the Temple to watch the procession. I wrote a poem based on memories of that *Perahera* in 1972, published I think in *The New York Review of Books*. But I had not returned to this country since I had left it at the age of seven in 1935. There was a terrible malaria epidemic just before I left and many of my memories were of fear: fear of being bitten by a mosquito and catching malaria or dengue fever, which I did catch, or of being bitten by a snake. And it was scary.

We understood and were proud that the island belonged to us, but we knew we did not belong here. That was made very clear. We were here for the good of the people, whom we were trying to help so that they could, eventually, govern themselves. But that might take rather a long time, we were led to believe. And Ceylon was, in fact, one of the best governed colonies in the British Empire. We also believed that the natives, some of whom were enormously rich – far richer than my family – were ever so lucky that we had conquered them, not the Germans, the Dutch, or the Portuguese. And we had already arranged for them to govern themselves, eventually!

BK: Can you explain a little more about your decision to return here permanently in 2007?

RM: When I was an infant, six weeks after I was born in my grandfather's very old house on the Mayo side of the Galway border near Kilmaine, between Tuam and Ballinrobe, I was brought out to Ceylon on an ocean liner through the Suez Canal, taking three weeks to reach Colombo, with children and nannies on one deck, parents on another. The first visit I don't remember because at the age of two, we returned to Ireland where my first memories begin. But we came out again when I was four, and there my Ceylon memories start. And they were full of fear, so much so that I didn't want to come back. My father never came back after he left in 1942, having suffered too much from heat, malaria, a lot of loneliness, anxiety, and separation. My mother said to a journalist in Colombo in 1985, 'Being married to someone in the colonial service in those days was very sad because you were always saying "goodbye", either to your husband or to your children.' I came back with my mother to Sri Lanka in 1984, almost fifty years after we had left Ceylon in 1935; and, for the first time in my life, I realised that I had had an incredibly happy childhood in this beautiful country. When the plane circled over Negombo and I saw the palm trees, and the lagoons, and the beach, and we landed, I felt I would like to kiss the ground. It was a wave of love and joy that arose from within me that I never knew was there. It was quite extraordinary. From there on, I thought that some of my heart is here in this country and I would like not to lose that.

I never felt the same about South Africa. I had been living on and off with or near my daughter Emily in South Africa and I decided that South Africa was no country for old men. People were being murdered every day for their cell phone, or a bit of jewellery. So when I reached the age of eighty in 2007, I thought that this is the time I should move, because of my second childhood, if you like. But I knew that the Sri Lankan people – the Sinhalese and the Tamils and the Muslim minority, who live here – are extremely kind to the old and to foreigners. I had formed friendships here on long visits from 1984 onwards. So seven years ago I moved.

BK: Can you tell us a little about the inspiration behind your 1989 book *The Mirror Wall* which is based on poems translated or adapted from Old Sinhala, the language at the root of modern Sinhala, which is spoken by the majority population here?

RM: Ashley Halpé, a very good friend who died last year, introduced me to the Sigiri Graffiti on which my versions were based. Ashley was a poet who had published English versions of thirty of these ancient Sinhala poems. He was a greatly admired Professor of English at the old University of Ceylon, which became the University of Peradeniya. That's about twelve kilometres from where I am living now in a valley of paddy fields and wooded hills. Ashley encouraged me, generously, to do my own versions, which, to my surprise, won the Poetry Book Society Translation Award in 1989. I didn't know Old Sinhala or even modern Sinhalese. But a Sinhala professor vetted all my versions and corrected or approved them as true to the spirit and wit of the original, particularly the wit.

I had great joy sitting on a cushion on a tiled floor in an empty, unfurnished room near Kandy, with a mongoose playing in the jungle outside, and a Buddhist Temple, on the other, making a lot of noise on Poya days. I had three huge volumes in front of me and a notebook in my hand: Paranavitana's double volume transcripts and translations and study of the Sigiri Graffiti; and the Sanskrit dictionary by Monier-Williams, who, in the nineteenth century, travelled all around India collecting words and their historical usages. An incredible work. It's like an encyclopedia! Each word having multiple meanings with examples going far back into Indian poetry, religion and mythology.

The poems from Sigiriya, the Lion Rock, in the centre of the island, were inscribed with a stylus on the highly-polished plaster of a parapet wall on the walkway going up to the top of the rock. It's a monolith, absolutely in the centre of the island, six hundred feet high and with marble steps and pathways all the way to the top. It was a sacred site. In the fifth or sixth century, a king – who was a parricide – had built a palace on top with tanks for collecting rainwater. He had created one of the finest water gardens in the whole of Asia! And he had painters – artists – painting frescoes, painted fresh on plaster – if you made a mistake, it stayed – in a grotto, on the side of the rock, about three hundred feet up. At one time, there were supposed to be five hundred beautiful images of women, who were either cloud nymphs – Apsaras – or wives of the king or concubines. Visitors, hundreds of years later, were speculating: who are these women? If they were his wives, why hadn't they jumped off the rock and killed themselves when he died? They must be whores! Some of the visitors had fallen in love with them and would regret that when they spoke, the women wouldn't answer! Other visitors were puritanical. It's thought that the period when King Kashyapa – the parricide – ruled was a period when *Mahāyāna* Buddhism predominated. But the tendency in Sri Lanka was for the *Theravāda* Buddhists' beliefs to predominate, and they were the puritans, and still are. I had to add detail and location to these poems. Writers of graffiti on the Mirror Wall at Sigiriya didn't have to do that because the people who would be reading the poem would see what everything looked like around them. So I tried to add the sort of information a reader would need who had never been to Sigiriya.

My favourite poem from the collection is one in which I discovered a word 'lola' in old Sinhala that means 'tossed about' or 'tossing about', closely related to a Sanskrit word 'lolita'. Nabokov may have chosen the name with knowledge of its perfectly appropriate etymology. Here is the poem:

A nectar-soaked bee
          tickled pink
      came out of his shell
                and tossing about
            with no restraint
    got deeply into a flower.

Humming all day long
      in her short gummy filaments,
          captive to joy
                that never stopped,
          by sunset he was biting
    the lotus to let him out.

BK: One feels that you have conveyed something of the essence of Sri Lanka in your work even without mastering the Sinhala language. But when you returned in the 1980s to the island, the language politics on the island had changed, of course. How did these later visits influence your poems with Sri Lankan settings?

RM: I confess, as I have said, that I didn't learn Sinhalese when I came back in 1984. I was too old. My father, when he came in 1910 to this country as a cadet in the Ceylon Civil Service, had two years in which to learn Sinhalese or Sinhala, and to pass a stiff exam in it, so that he could conduct all his business in Sinhala, if need be. Then he had a year in which to learn Tamil, which was rather less time. He was posted to Mullaitivu which is now an infamous place because it got into the news as the place where the last stand of the LTTE Tiger terrorists took place, where they were wiped out. In 1913, my father was appointed the assistant government agent there; it was his first posting. He had to buy a motorbike and go into the immense jungle, to see if trouble was going on. Anyway, my father was a very, very good linguist and I was never that. I remember, in my childhood, that we didn't speak Sinhalese or Tamil, although I was told afterwards that as a very small child, aged two and a half, I could talk to the servants! The great land-owning families, like the Bandaranaikes, spoke English to each other, and Sinhala or Tamil to their servants. That was how it was in the colonial period and then the Sinhala prime minister, S.W.R.D. Bandaranaike, whose father had worn a top hat and sat in the royal box at Ascot with King George V, abolished English as a national language in 1956 and closed the race course in Nuwara Eliya.

It was my friend, the late Barbara Epstein in New York, who suggested to me in 1971 that it might be better if I wrote some poems about my childhood in Ceylon before I went there, because as soon as I went back, my memories would be overlaid by new sights and sounds and culture. And so I wrote the Ceylon poems in *High Island* in 1971, 1972 and 1973. These are flashbacks to my childhood. And in the matter of language, I was fascinated by how there could be a connection between the sound you made – like 'beat'– and the meaning, and how, if you repeated a word often enough, these two might get disconnected. We heard the strange sounds in our compound garden, made by the servants, while all the grand Sinhala ladies spoke English to us. These notions gave me the poem 'Coppersmith', the name for a bird, a crimson barbet, which is a kind of woodpecker found in Sri Lanka.

COPPERSMITH

A temple tree grew in our garden in Ceylon.
We knew it by no other name.
The flower, if you turned it upside down,
Looked like a dagoba with an onion dome.
A holy perfume
Stronger than the evil tang of betel-nut
Enticed me into its shade on the stuffiest afternoon,

Where I stood and listened to the tiny hammer-stroke
Of the crimson coppersmith perched above my head,
His *took took took*
And his *tonk tonk tonk*
Were spoken in a language I never understood:
And there I began to repeat
Out loud to myself an English word such as beat beat beat,

Till hammering too hard I lost the meaning in the sound
Which faded and left nothing behind,
A blank mind,
The compound spinning round,
My brain melting, as if I'd stood in the sun
Too long without a topee and was going blind,
Till I and the bird, the word and the tree, were one.

BK: In your memoir, *The Kick*, you describe some of the political violence in recent years in Sri Lanka. Can you tell us more about how these events influenced your view of the island in your work?

RM: The country has now, we all hope, put its troubles behind it. At the time when I returned with my mother, in November 1984, two civil wars were beginning – one in the north and another in the south. The one in the south was an extreme left-wing movement that believed in the annihilation of the bourgeoisie. It did not succeed, but it resulted in the deaths of about ten thousand supporters of the government at the time, and, in the course of reprisals – and in the elimination of the JVP – about fifty or sixty thousand people died. We don't know to this day whether they were members of the JVP, or just suspected of being such.

My poem 'Sri Lanka' is a sonnet written after I'd finished *The Price of Stone* and had come back to Sri Lanka in 1984. I'd been studying the country's history, its different names and sufferings under different rulers, and its final rejoicing in Buddhist-ruled independence. It is the voice of Sri Lanka which speaks, the spirit of the country describing itself. I refer to 'leonine blood' because the lion is the national symbol, the symbol of the ancestral Sinhala people, and the word 'resplendent' comes from the word 'Lanka' which means 'resplendent' in the Sinhala language. But the poem also suggests that Sri Lanka is a country that suffers, and suffers from all sorts of misfortune.

SRI LANKA

Being nearly heart-shaped made me seem a ham
    On early spice trade navigators' charts
    Tinctured with cinnamon, peppered with forts,
To be eaten up under a strong brand name
Like Taprobane, Serendip, Tenarisim –
    Copper-palmed lotus island slave resorts –
    And I succumbed to lordly polished arts
That cut me down to seem a white king's gem,
A star sapphire teardrop India shed
    On old school maps, a lighthouse of retorts
Flashing from head to head. My leonine blood
Throbbed wildly when resplendent freedom came
    Mouthing pearl tropes with Pali counterparts,
Exalted, flawed; and made me seem as I am.

Several decades ago, the rulers decided that Sri Lanka must have a national tree and they chose the ironwood tree. And in 1989, at the height of the JVP crisis, particularly in the southern, central and western provinces, all of Sri Lanka, except the part that was Tamil occupied, there was chaos and mayhem. There had been an election where nobody could go out to vote, and yet, miraculously, a large majority was 'discovered' for the government. And I wrote the poem 'National Tree' after a visit to a very interesting arboretum near Dambulla. It was donated by its owner Sam Popham to the University of Peradeniya because he wanted it to be maintained as an arboretum. It was about five acres of low scrub jungle in which Sam had allowed the jungle to come up. Nature – the goddess – was allowed to grow. But Sam – the colonialist – decided which aspects of nature he liked and which he didn't. So any trees he didn't like, one of his five gardeners would be told to uproot it; and the trees he liked were allowed to thrive – like satinwood, and ironwood, and mahogany and teak, and so on.

NATIONAL TREE

The flowers of the ironwood
Last for a day.
Opening at sunrise
They fall when the sun goes down.

Their little white flags
With yellow hearts
Flutter in a state
Of carnival and terror.

Yesterday's petals
Lie beheaded on the ground.
There are buds in hiding:
Tomorrow these will explode.

Above the low scrub jungle
Seething in hot air
The young leaves turn
Transparently blood-red.

A king cobra demon
Stays hoodwinking on top
The ironwood grows high
Exuding festivity.

One of the wonderful things about Sri Lanka is the capacity of the people for joy, and for joy expressed in carnival. The carnival went on and on and on all through the terror – the terror, on the one hand, from the left-wing killer extremists, and on the other, from the death squads that were unleashed against them by the government. The carnival went on and on. And that's a wonderful thing, the spirit of the people survived in those who outlived the terror. Why was the horror ignored in the western media? I think because it coincided with Tiananmen Square, and the media like to focus on one world-class atrocity at a time.

At that time, I was staying in Kandy and every morning there were queues at the morgue of mothers and fathers and brothers and sisters seeing if their disappeared ones had turned up. A young friend of mine had been taken off the street. He disappeared. We heard that he had been dragged by five soldiers from a militia, or death squad, from door to door in five villages. In one of these I had stayed and written *The Mirror Wall* translations. He was beaten up and tortured and exhibited from door to door as a member of the JVP. Anura had stayed in his village because he knew he was innocent, but his friends had run away, because they were members of the JVP. That's all we know. His body was never found, no death certificate was ever issued to his mother, who went looking for trace of him from one police barracks or army camp to another.

I based the poem 'Death in Kandy' on notes I had written very rapidly at the time and I was not sure, really, whether it was a poem or not. Since I had had the good fortune to meet Dennis O'Driscoll with Julie O'Callaghan at the Kilkenny Festival of 1976, I had always asked for and taken his advice on any poem I had written. No one in the world could have been more generous with his precious time, and with his immense knowledge, supreme intelligence, and profound love of poetry than Dennis. He was my first and best reader, never growing impatient, always putting a finger on a weak word or line in such a kind way that a better word or line would soon come to my mind and gain his approval. He helped me revise one version after another of 'Death in Kandy', which he never thought was a good poem – borderline, if anything. At last he said, 'Put it in the book, if you like!', so I did.

His death numbed me into a shameful silence. I've never been able to write the elegy demanded of me – too old, perhaps – but others have written so well of his life and his poetry that his great warm personality, so deeply missed by his innumerable friends and admirers, will never be forgotten, nor will his poetry.

Nessa O'Mahony

SOUND AND VISIONS

Paddy Bushe, *On a Turning Wing* (Dedalus Press, 2016), €11.50.
Eleanor Hooker, *A Tug of Blue* (Dedalus Press, 2016), €11.50.
Claire Dyer, *Interference Effects* (Two Rivers Press, 2016) £9.99.

During a recent stay at Cill Rialaig in West Kerry, I listened to the poet Dairina Ní Chinnéide playing the ragged notes of 'Port na bPúcaí' on her tin whistle, and heard tell of how the tune was said to have originated from fairy music under the waves beating off the Blasket islands. I was reminded of that inextricable weaving of fable, art, and nature as I read Paddy Bushe's prize-winning collection *On a Turning Wing* (it won the *Irish Times* Poetry Now award in March 2017); the book, especially the opening sections, explores the theme of the eternal connection between the expressive arts, the natural landscape, and the people who inhabit it.

According to Bushe, art is not simply what it represents; it has an intrinsic quality of its own. The opening poem,'The Rolling Wave', which takes its title from a traditional air, depicts the solitary fiddler so immersed in the performance that it is hard to see where the musician finishes and the tune begins:

> So he played, not the tune itself but the tune
> Being itself. And the house played with him,
> Its timbers resonating like tightened strings,
>
> Until he stood, his bow still drawn across
> The still quivering air, in the new stillness
> Inside his music, unmoving, transformed.

The natural world is omnipresent; the poem tells of the 'wind in the birches that gave the valley / Its name and shaped its oldest stories'. That intimate connection between nature and art is also explored in 'Two Poems of Piping', where in the first section, the piper advises the apprentice to learn by feeling '*the turn the way a blackbird draws / A worm from the earth, taking the strain / Steadily until the worm yields*'. Bushe extends the metaphor beautifully, transforming the worm into an 'anchor rope' between teacher and student, and evoking that DNA chain of artistic apprenticeship.

Many of the early poems touch on artists' practices, whether it is the affectionate portrait of the painter Pauline Bewick at work – 'She shivered, deliciously, / And, taking colour and water onto her brush, //

Touched it to the parchment', or capturing the famous Japanese artist Hokusai's *Tama River* (in the poem of the same name), whose ferryman is 'angled / Hard against his pole to hold the bow steady // Through wind and current'. In many poems, Bushe explores representation; how we perceive and how tradition shapes our perception. For example, when responding to Waterville artist Jean Usher's painting of swallows, in the first section of 'Of Paint and Clay and Words: Two Poems', he evokes, along with the swallows, Hopkins' 'The Windhover': 'So much // To stir the *heart in hiding* and to tumblespin it'. He then continues by staking his claim for the role of poetry: 'I say that poetry also jinks, as through a portal / Into and out of itself, that it inscribes the sky'.

There are memorial poems, too; few of Bushe's generation are spared the loss of friends and fellow poetic travellers. His 'Postcard from Rome' contains this poignant evocation of Pearse Hutchinson:

> I thought of you in the hospital, frail
> And articulate as a threatened language,
> Enquiring as ever behind your darkening eyes.

There are also memorials to Seamus Heaney and the Russian poet Regina Derieva. But tradition is returned to constantly; the line stretches back to Amergin, whose poems Bushe translates here; they provide a neat linkage to an extended sequence denouncing the loss of arts funding for Tech Amergin, his local Waterville arts centre. Homer might have made the *Iliad* from such a local row, and it is clearly an issue close to the poet's heart, yet for this reader the juxtaposition of natural lyric and political polemic didn't work. These angry poems (as with the political caricatures in the final section of the book) feel blunted compared to the finely honed pieces that open the collection and continue throughout. For me, Bushe's genius is in his ability to observe and capture the mutable, whether it be in music or visual art or in the constantly changing land and seascape of his beloved Southwest Kerry. And there is, thankfully, ample evidence of that genius on show in this collection.

If the wild Atlantic figures prominently in Bushe's poetry, then an inland expanse of water (Lough Derg) features in Eleanor Hooker's. Hooker is a long-time resident of Dromineer, Co Tipperary, (not to mention a regular crew member for the RNLI), so the lake, and water-borne imagery, are a constant presence in her second collection, A *Tug of Blue*. That her imagination takes a frequent surreal turn is evident in the opening poem 'Weathering', where the personified Rain is upstairs, rinsing 'a naked bulb that hung itself / on white wire. *It ran out of light*, / she says, spreading her fall'. In 'Upended', Rain acts more naturalistically – 'pushes under slates / and spits on the floor' – but the sense of disquiet pervades, the feeling of being trapped and abandoned at the same time:

> I am a solitary creature who
> is told not to be a solitary
> creature, to let others in.
>
> Into what, I wonder,
> there's just me and an echo
> in here ...

Omens are everywhere: the crows in 'Escape Route' issuing 'their thin black sermons'; the ravens in 'To Stay Going' who torment or guard the poem's protagonist, depending on whose account you believe. He is a Wordsworthian solitary who 'was cursed from the day / he stole those raven's eggs'. The dead calf floating to the shore of the lake in 'A Weather Eye' is another portent; the fact that it has disappeared by sunrise, still prey to the larger forces of the lake, is even more disquieting: 'Wind had / changed, so water took her elsewhere.'

This sense of being haunted, or of living in waking nightmares, recurs in many poems. The doppelgänger, in the poem of the same name, who hums Prokofiev, reappears in 'Mirrored', 'her song the sound of a heavy body / dragging itself, deadly, up the stairs'. It is a risky strategy by Hooker to offer so many surrealistic poems without once capitulating to naturalism. It asks the reader to surrender herself to the downward momentum into subliminality. But Hooker persuades us through the sheer beauty of her imagery, for all its Poe-like darkness. Here for example, in 'Nailing Wings to the Dead', is a survivor from a blight-filled world preparing for the end:

> "This dark stain,
> passed kiss to kiss-stained
> fevered mouth,
> blights love, is pulsed
> by death-watch beetle's
> tick, timing our decay."

There are rare lighter moments: the guardian angel from the poem of the same name cursing when spreading his wings; or the mocking self-portrait in 'Light Air', in which the poet abandons her reading of *Sense and Sensibility* to respond to the lifeboat's call:

> In modest nightgown –
> (thirty yards of Georgian cotton) – and husband's gum boots, (O no troglodyte

am I), I took myself to Station, then quickly moved when frowns
from fellow crew outlined how nightgown, 'gainst a stout searchlight, reveals.

But the tone is predominantly sombre, as if a lifetime's exposure to the harshness of life by water had darkened her vision. The longest poem in the collection is 'The Shout', a gripping and wonderfully sustained account of a lifeboat call-out where the outcome, for once, is favourable. But elsewhere we are reminded of the fragility of the boundary between life and death, even in pre-natal states, as in 'The Sea' with its wonderfully strange conjuring of the child in the womb:

Full of the sea.
At spring tide
and gibbous moon
it splashes the rocky
outcrops of his skull,
spills out of caves
onto his face.
That is the sea
washing his face.

Hooker's gift is a troubling one; one is charmed and haunted by her poetry in equal measure.

We return to more mundane concerns in *Interference Effects*, which is Claire Dyer's second poetry collection; her first was published in 2013 and she also previously published three novels. That narrative predilection runs through many of the poems in her new book; the tone is chatty, the language visual and original as she charts her quotidian existence.

A family holiday is evoked in 'On the Pier', where the 'air was stitched with salt and gulls' and caught mackerel 'twisted on the deck like tinsel', whilst in 'What Lies Within' we are shown 'the fizz-torn dazzle of a street lamp'. In 'Lost and Found' we are brought on a reverse trip back to the source of the unnamed item that has been misplaced, which is found 'by the till // next to the two-for-ones / flapping in a dying fish sort of way'. The cryptic is a common strategy in Dyer's work; frequently those everyday depictions take a surreal twist as in 'What's Left Is This', where:

... by the cashpoint
inside Lloyds Bank a man
in a blue coat takes
my collar bone, plucks

it straight out.

Further amputations take place in the line at Tesco's, and in a lunch-time café, leaving the titular climax of 'one marvellous heart', which somehow doesn't quite satisfy the poem's quirky build-up.

Quirkiness is a matter of taste and for me it is perhaps the weak point of this collection; Dyer can be highly original, but she is so busy telling it slant that one occasionally wishes for a poem that offers us a straighter, more profound account of the perils of modern living. She comes closest to this in poems like 'The Label Maker', where the poem's subject 'carries a pop-up house in a velveteen bag, / is bald, shameless, has obsidian eyes', and applies his pernicious labels to the homeless and hopeless of society; or in 'Perspective', where the speaker 'wanted not an idea of beauty, // but the blade of beauty against my throat'.

Dyer provides us with many startling images but sometimes one wishes she had paid greater attention to the sonic aspects of poetry; perhaps the prose writer is more interested in the visual than in sound, as lines such as these from 'Don't Tell Me I've Got It Wrong' seem to suggest:

> It was hot,
> heat rising from the roofs of cars,
>
> heat solid and surprising
> that made warm the pavements and the walls.

There is less music in Dyer's work than is audible in Bushe's or Hooker's poetry, but her eye for the memorable image is undeniable.

Moya Cannon

AT DOGS' BAY

This winter's storms have chewed off
half a row of dunes
have revealed a line of midden –
a charcoal stroke across a page of clean time
burnt winkles, burnt bones, burnt wood —
hearths smoored forever by the tail-swish
of some pre-historic hurricane.

And above the midden line,
in the fresh sand-cliff,
is a crooked line of burrows –
a new city,
a twittering, cliffside pueblo,
a lively Petra,
where sand-martins,
rested after their Sahara crossing,
are swallowed up and shot out
to scribe the sky
with quick calligraphy,
jubilant diagonals.

Patrick FitzSymons

HUNTERS

I saw them from the kitchen,
spattered cars and a white van grumbling
on the lane, Sunday morning,

and answered the knock
as he sucked the shining salt from his fingers,
plunging them again in the Cheese & Onion.

"Any danger of a bit of hunting?"
Belfast accent, seventy miles from home,
a statement of a question.

Nearby, others peered from below
muddy arches on windscreens, while unseen
dogs yapped and scrabbled.

There were saplings in the fields below,
many nicked by hares and barely escaping
the mat of uncut winter grass.

But, "No," I said.
Silence then, and a tilt of the head as he turned
side on, closed a bloodshot eye.

Engines revved and they left, snapping
like fireworks on the gravel
to call on my neighbour. Maybe he had chickens

and trouble with a fox, or believed
those badger TB stories, but for the next hour
I came and went from the window,

searching for shapes coming through the gorse,
intent on killing something,
whether I wanted to or not.

Caroline Price

SIGNAL, CROMER

The explosion sends gulls
arching away, their cries inaudible.
A car back-firing, no more than that
but he trembles, waiting, hearing the feet
in his mind still, men running, one throwing
aside a half-mended net, another
swinging round from the pots on the quay,
two more bursting out of the Albion
on the corner to be met by the boys
from the butcher's and the fishmonger's
and the young lads from further out, hatless
and breathless, thudding this way
down Jetty Street past the church and sharp left
to the sea front, he's with them now, two
at a time up the steps to the pier
and thundering along it, shaking the planks
to the shed at the far end where they hardly
slow down to fumble their jackets from the racks
and into the boat, propellers spinning in air
as the doors gape open, as they plunge towards water
and rise again through a bow-wave of spray –
that's the last he remembers, he was still
fastening his coat, his eyes
on the distance as they rose and rose again.

Enda Wyley

SOMEWHERE ELSE

To discard the city – to let it
go for a while, to go where
you have never been before
on a mid March day –
is a perfect thing to do.
The mist is rising and soon
the countryside speeds by –
golden fields and rolling green
emerging from the haze.

⋆

At the edge of the gardens
you lean against the car door,
smoking a cigar, waiting.
You are here to let me off
about my business –
burnt house to see
for the first time,
the monkey-puzzle
avenue to crane to.
There were the high grasses
of your student days
in the Iveagh Gardens
but now, years on,
these gardens
and the storm that ravaged
and has us standing here.

⋆

The white cat knew all
that was before us
when it slinked
from the valley of Gabhra
and sauntered across the lane,
then heated itself
by the fires of the bothy huts,
later gorging

on the glass house's melons.
It had its own way
but knew when the time
was right, to cross before us,
a steady white on the road
we took back to the city –
great friend dying,
the front door banging,
the wind in the east rising
to fell trees that have stood
for thousands of years.

*

I wake to your words
falling with the rain
and cup them in my hand.
Such short, simple things
with no punctuation
to bind them tight
and yet their meaning
is caught in the flow
of thought on the screen.
A beep and I reply,
imagining your hands,
somewhere else,
reaching up to catch
my words back to you.
A house destroyed,
a river path overgrown,
conservatory glass
all shattered, a walled
garden locked, the past
drowning, but this text
grasps at the future,
is what was and cannot
be forgotten.

Prayag Ray

PRINCE AND PRINCESS OF WALES IN INDIA

archive film, 1905

Seven ghostly men step off a boat
in seven ghostly costumes,
bananas, octopuses, and pies
on their heads. A woman dressed
like a wedding cake follows, lilting
florally off the boat.

They stride across the ghats,
carrying swords, trumpets; the ladies,
fans. One fellow is all in black, a black
tureen upside down on his head.
The lack of sound disturbs you.

You wonder if this is all it takes:
an absurd pageant, coats starched and
skins lighter, to make the black
fellows bow. A handful of decisive actors
with banana hats, and
an idea of infinite ascendancy.

Camera pans to the right –
featureless rows of turbans bounce along.
A couple of camels. Black men,
black horses, white men, black horses,
some important people being fanned.

Dominic Fisher

JET TRAILS

after Stanley Kunitz
from Alexander Blok

Streetlight, roofline, jet trail, plane.
All day the news has not been good.
You know this so I won't explain
and I'm not confident I could.

Sometimes the atmosphere confirms
that love and colour are the same.
The stars are drowned, the sun returns.
Streetlight, roofline, jet trail, plane.

Jessica Traynor

VARIOUS GHOSTS

David Butler, *All The Barbaric Glass* (Doire Press, 2017), €12.
Susan Millar DuMars, *Bone Fire* (Salmon Poetry, 2016), €12.
Afric McGlinchey, *Ghost of the Fisher Cat* (Salmon Poetry, 2016), €12.

In *Waiting for Godot*, Vladimir and Estragon contemplate the condition of the dead with the exchange: 'To have lived is not enough for them [...] To be dead is not enough for them.' This passage of dialogue captures something of our anxiety about the next world. Where are the dead now? What do they think? Is poetry, perhaps, a language that can capture something of their world? Each of these three new collections is concerned in its own way with an attempt to probe the membrane of the next world; to see if there's any give.

David Butler's *All the Barbaric Glass,* which directly references the above Beckett passage, is a collection of littoral and liminal spaces, inhabiting a cold coastal world from which the poet contemplates his father's slow deterioration. This is a collection of mercurial weather, cold waterscapes, and rusted iron; the poet watches this unforgiving landscape with curiosity, seeking clues as to what may come. In the collection's opening poem, 'Breaking', this seemingly bleak landscape is set up as a contrast to the cold, narcissistic world of media; although the seascape can be cruel, it is a landscape whose cycles mirror our own and whose familiarity allows us to

> ... listen to the gossip of waves,
> the hunger, the blood-course;
> the seabird's ululation
> across a desolate sunset.

A sequence of poems about the poet's father's death roots the mood of the collection concretely in an experience which has become sadly ubiquitous in recent years; the slow loss of a parent to dementia. Here, Butler is at his best, using precise and economical language to channel the not inconsiderable emotion of the situation into heartfelt and direct poems that don't shy away from the more piteous aspects of death in a nursing home. 'These are the Dead Days' takes us 'Into the nappy warmth, the air / clammy with the taint of incontinence / [...] to watch the slow descent to where he sits: / your father a child again'. In 'Father', a litany of questions creates the air of a weary catechism, with the poet's interest in mythology inflecting the prayer-like address of the last lines: 'Forgive us / this daily trespass through your threadless maze.'

Butler's poetry approaches the emotional realm through the lens of a keen and considered intellect, and this is reflected both in the subject matter and in the tone of language used throughout the collection. There are times when the use of polysyllabic (if always well-chosen) adjectives can threaten to clutter the rhythm of a reflective poem, but poems such as 'Snow', 'Oghma's Gift', and 'Icarus' demonstrate a clarity which allows the reader to share the poet's sense of revelation. Butler's use of archetypes is deft and understated, and, in 'Icarus', his re-imagining of the well-known myth sheds new light on the father-son relationship:

> Now, from beyond the horizon
> I allow him his bar-room story
> of how I plunged headlong
> into the labyrinth of waves.
>
> Plumage and wax are concealed.
> I'll not rise against his testament.

Susan Millar DuMars' *Bone Fire* is also concerned with matters of mortality. Her poetry, influenced by the directness of the American tradition, comes as a breath of fresh air in a wider Irish scene where the tone and delivery of poems can still occasionally echo the liturgy. In 'Meet You', an old relationship with its misunderstandings, near-misses, and fleeting moments of tenderness is evoked through a one-sided dialogue which pulls the reader into the poem's intimacies with well-chosen details, such as a funny meditation on the poet's dislike of confrontation: 'Oh my god, you said / if you can't / send back a milkshake'.

These are poems that deal with personal loss, but also with wider conflict. Not only do they delve into family history, but into the history of Millar DuMars' twin homes – Ireland and the USA – with fertile results. 'Thirst' cleverly and clearly explores the idea of trauma as something that can be passed on at a genetic level. The poet paints a surreal and terrifying picture of a Belfast bar explosion witnessed by her grandfather, the experience of which has ghosted itself onto the poet's limbs: 'He smiles at me / and I feel the cold caress, / in my two hands, of a glass.' The poet concludes that although the details of the story my be apocryphal, an indelible mark has been left:

> This tale passed down
> of you shrugging off
> a Belfast bomb
> is all I've inherited –
>
> that, and this thirst.

A lament for America's youth, 'Stripes and Stars' deftly accomplishes the tricky task of commenting on the alienation experienced by young men in the military, juxtaposing familiar societal symbols with affecting moments of personal dread: 'the flagpole at night clanks *lonely, lonely* / and you shove your dresser against the door'.

The past weighs heavily on the poet. There is a sense throughout the collection that the time we move through is cyclical rather than linear, and we would be foolish to imagine that it doesn't occasionally bunch like a rug to trip us. The collection's title poem, which makes reference to the Celtic practice of burning the bones of the dead, is one of the poems that acknowledge this:

> Smoke that winds
> around my wrist
> becomes your hand.
>
> And you won't let go.

Afric McGlinchey's *Ghost of the Fisher Cat* both haunts and is haunted by Paris. Taking as its unifying symbol the ghost of a cat who is said to have been the familiar of a seventeenth-century Parisian apothecary, it uses this tale as a jumping off point for a series of poems which deal, like Millar DuMars' work, with the personal and the historical.

This is an ambitious collection whose magpie tendencies are woven together by the fisher cat which pads through each of its five sections. McGlinchey's voice differs again from the other two poets, with its focus on the lushly sensual. She luxuriates in the possibilities of language, and her readers will enjoy the riches on offer here. In poems such as 'Ode to an Itinerant Cat', the simple pleasure of a cat's purring is described in unforgettable terms: 'slipping at last into my lap, like rain-spill into a river, / your purring, electric as fences, vibrating through skin'. In 'A Matter of Persistence' she resurrects the ghost of a cat for us with such vividness that we share the disbelief of the poem's baffled witnesses, two lads sharing a smoke after a rain shower:

> Next thing, he sees a frisson becoming
> solid in the street; a bristling, vivid, green-eyed
> density, with every double-take!
> His disbelief is stalled
> when she caterwauls, tail a victory flag.

There's an arch sense of humour at work in these poems; often the hint that beneath the poems' surface elegance, there's a stifled peal of laughter. McGlinchey avoids earnestness and we smile along with her at the comic vagaries of history. In 'Familiar', the rumour and intrigue surrounding Dom Perlet, owner of the fisher cat, are evoked in a poem that ventriloquizes the voices of the time:

> Look – there's his cat! Have you observed how
> they walk through the city, uncannily close,
> as though figure and shadow? Or witch and familiar!

The poem eventually reveals the bravado and bluster to be empty, as the speaker's listeners back away in fear from the prospect of drowning the cursed cat: 'Hey! Don't look at me! Aren't you following?'

Outside of the shade-world of Parisian alleyways, McGlinchey reveals a wider world reflecting the poet's experience of travel and a life lived between Ireland, Zimbabwe, Paris, and London. In 'I Is Not Always Me', the voice of a migrant in a new country is channelled in poignant terms, reflecting on the profit and loss offered by the adoption of a new language:

> I think of how a foreign language percolates
> your own, until its idioms even permeate your dreams.
> That's not just acquisition, but erosion too.

The only criticism I might level at these three collections has more to do with the challenging nature of Irish poetry publication, operating bravely in perennially straitened circumstances, than the individual collections. In the case of the McGlinchey and the Butler books, both approaching fifty poems, I wondered if perhaps the inclusion of fewer poems might have allowed each book's gems to shine all the brighter? But what are poets and poetry presses to do when finances dictate that many emerging or mid-career poets must wait four or five years between collections, during which time a substantial body of work may be building up? In any case, these three collections, published by dedicated publishers Salmon Poetry and Doire Press, serve as a testament to the imaginative health of contemporary Irish poetry.

Chris Preddle

MAKER

Jacqueline the maker,
hauler in
of megaliths to Mag
Hill, heeler in
of violas blue violas,
maker of values,

turned there
on the turning hill
as another era
turned on its heel,
and what had formed her
turned from her.

Virgil sang: I'm Homer
but prescient. Roland and Aude
have been as you are, out of humour
in a new world order.

Be humbler in Europe. I foresaw
Rome and Christ, both gone.
You won't see what you sorrow for.
New things begin.

Mary O'Donnell

MUSE

I want to be stolen
by this two-legged creature,
not quite human.

He lives in the wild brackens
beyond the garden.

I must stay alert,
alone, resist the cosmetic clatter
of an evening of too many useless acts.

Pointless to tempt him with inscribed saucers
of scallops, marbled blue cheese,
or the Omega of bone marrow.

His appetite is not sated on such
fine produce. As he springs silently,
raw as a goat, through the rime frost
and a chink in the porch window,
I inhale the funk of him,
sense his stealth, have known it
all my life.

He stands at my back, caresses my arm,
the one that cramps with the pain of staying put,
his one silver hoof tapping a line, a rhyme,
on the floorboards.

He scarcely whispers, yet, bothered
by his absence these sullen months,
I hear him clearly.

Hush now, (such sibilant breaths),
I have broken the fences, the safe arbours
that restrained you, have torn down
the walls
that bound you to silence.

I twitch to answer, accepting
his hand-curl around mine. In an instant,
our fingers shift across the moonlit desk.

Matthew Rice

BEYOND

Given though I am to lying
in a darkened room,
the fact that the black-out drape
refuses to fall to the base of the window
renders it no less culpable
for the letterbox of light
which posts itself through the dark;
the same foot of light
that holds the half-chewed
plum-skin by the dresser in reverence,
lending weight to the notion
nothing is beyond meaning;
the very same foot of light that
broke upon the lighthouse steps
the other night as I was focused
on shaping the gum in my mouth
to the globed earth;
the very same which,
a quarter of a century ago,
widened across my bedroom carpet
framing my father, book in hand;
the very same foot of light that
travelled beyond us then,
beyond the darkened room.

Stephen Sexton

ROMANTIC, GEOMANTIC, ANTIC

Maura Dooley, *The Silvering* (Bloodaxe Books, 2016), £9.95.
Paula Meehan, *Geomantic* (Dedalus Press, 2016), €12.50.
Matthew Sweeney, *Inquisition Lane* (Bloodaxe Books, 2015), £9.95.

'Silvering' is the process by which a piece of glass is treated in order to make it reflective. Maura Dooley's latest collection uses this metaphor to position its speaker in relation to the world: rather than allowing matters of politics and history to pass by unremarked upon, these are poems of witness and reflection. Light itself constitutes another theme, and consequently, there are, for Dooley, various ways of looking at objects as well as the environments that contain them. The opening poem, the Forward Prize-shortlisted 'Cleaning Jim Dine's Heart', is an ekphrastic poem that takes as its subject the cover image of the book:

> In the afternoon sunlight at deCordova sculpture park
> she is on the top rung of a pair of steps cleaning a big
> dark heart. And it has everything in it, this heart. Twice.
> Even the coffee pot I brought back in hand luggage ...

It's some variation of this coffee pot embedded in Dine's sculpture that takes on a central role in the poem, invoking a home in London, in which it blows up. Dine's sculpture contains too, says the speaker, 'worn out shoes, rope, / the hammers and saws of a life together, coffee'. This way of looking – of interpreting the world and finding oneself reflected in it is a powerful aspect of Dooley's collection.

A pair of poems remember General Elections: the speaker's 'first vote, maiden voyage' in 'Life and Land, Thursday May 3rd 1979', and the most recent election but one, 'Grass, Thursday May 7th 2015', whose interplay of fury, frustration and optimism is short enough to reproduce here:

> The dirt beneath your feet?
> You stand on it, grind it underheel,
> you spit on it.
>
> The dirt beneath your feet?
> It carries seed, it nourishes,
> it rises green.

The collection features two short sequences of poems. The first is a set of three poems whose titles begin with 'In a dream…' followed by a fourth poem in which (no dream) 'He buys her a hot whiskey'. The collection's second sequence, four poems titled 'From the Album', describe photographs; particularly the complicated kind of presence photographs possess. In the first of these, subtitled '*At Cliveden*', 'the picture slides / into blankness which might be / where he is now, quiet, a little apart, / just a stone's throw away from us'.

Like many of the best poems, these too ask what poems are useful for. In 'In a dream he is still busy', 'waiting falls / on her like rain, a fine mist, a softness / she finds words for, *haar, smirr,* / stupid poetry words'. In 'And Afterwards', hearing from a taxi driver how 'the old man, / Christopher Thornton, gave him a pair of boots / with blades and told him how in 1919 he'd skated,' the speaker wonders 'what it all adds up to: the ice, / the pond the gentry calls a lake, the waiting blades, all this telling'. Who knows, is probably the answer. Or the answer is to do what the old man says, should ice so thick come again: '*make sure you make good use of these*'.

Paula Meehan's *Geomantic* is a work of divination. Geomancy, Wikipedia says, 'interprets markings on the ground or the patterns formed by tossed handfuls of soil, rocks, or sand'. Clairvoyance is only ever about the present, and this collection's 81 nine-syllable, nine-line, definite article poems ('The Moons', 'The Fascinator', 'The Pearl'), are less about telling the future than understanding the world as it now appears. The poems' titles function as questions to which the 9 x 9 structure – operating as a kind of scrim or filter over the world – discerns an answer. The book begins not necessarily with earth but with the moon's measure of time on earth, in elegant and incantatory lines:

> night moon and day moon, moon in eclipse,
> slender new moon in the winter sky,
> and full harvest moon — a golden ball;
> moon of my first breath, my mother's death ...
>
> – 'THE MOONS'

The matters of the present are many: there are love poems, poems of history and technology, of childhood and nationhood. A run of four poems comments on the legacy of 1916: 'Nineteen sixty-six, eleven years / old, let me die for Ireland I prayed', says the speaker in 'The Child I Was'. In 'The Graves at Arbour Hill', 'Ireland' is mentioned three times, 'Irish' twice. 2016 seemed like the year of semantic saturation, and this poem reads as a reassertion of a vow on one hand, and on the other, as a caution against claiming the future: 'there'll come a day I'll be dust in wind, / Irish dust in Irish wind, a hundred / and a hundred million years from now'.

This seventh collection features, like Meehan's other collections, many poems concerned with the craft of language and, particularly, the gulf between signifier and signified. 'The Gift', a deathbed recollection, casts the two-year-old speaker in a garden as a prelapsarian Adam or Eve who commits the valuable act of telling us not what things are, but how they are:

> Like a queen who rules all she surveys
> I'm saying *nice nice nice* as I wave
> to bee, fly, worm, wasp, bird, to the blue
> cloudless sky, at home in creation …

The gift is the recollection, but the facility of language too, and the possibility of its making 'order from chaos' ('The Moon Rose Over an Open Field'). Chaos is, in its earliest sense, the void from which matter would emerge. For Meehan, it's the wash of information and experience she will render into her poems. The process of divination, whether literal or metaphorical, is the intellect that refines the entirety of sensory experience, ultimately resolving it into language.

Matthew Sweeney has no doubt been an important influence for a recent generation of poets of a surrealist bent. In *Inquisition Lane*, his eleventh collection, the deft, energetic, and strange poems he is known for are graceful and moving and silly in the best way. All poems are imaginative in some sense or another, but – in much of Irish poetry especially – poems are often imagination-plated: a flourish of surrealism animates a fairly plausible autobiographical text. In Sweeney's poems, we are frequently faced with unresolvable fables, and comic narratives that seem to proceed from nowhere else but their title, or opening line or image.

The book's opening poem, 'The Dream House', articulates in distinct details the distance between image and thing, between want and actualisation:

> Inside the house was a circular
> staircase with yellow mosaics
> leading to the inner, upper haven.
> There was no furniture downstairs.
> There was no one living there.

It's not clear if the dream house was so because no one lived there, or that no one lived there because it was a figment of the imagination. Death is a recurring theme, and the book's several elegies are vivacious; 'Into the Air' for Seamus Heaney remembers 'high choral singing, meant to lead / you through the diamond-studded gates / of heaven, where you'd sign books for God'. 'Cloud Communication' for Dennis O'Driscoll, and the lengthier concluding poem 'Co-Author' for John

Hartley Williams, likewise address their subjects personally, doing that thing that gives elegies their special power – speaking to the dead.

Sweeney's poems always seem to celebrate the peculiar physics of what can happen in poems, which is anything. In 'The Poem You've Been Waiting For', a blind dog is 'walking alongside a slithering rattlesnake / on North Main Street in Cork'. 'The One-eyed Philosopher of Katmandu' chastises his parrot companion: 'Typical of a bird, / he said, to be so sure of great death's gender.' By some kind of paradox, what might be non sequiturs in the work of another poet are perfectly sequential according to the logic of these poems: something has to happen, so anything may as well. This is perhaps most evident in the opening lines of poems such as 'The Beauty Institute' ('The Beauty Institute was closed / so I went to the harbour'), and 'The Mallow Races' ('Have you ever been to the Mallow Races? / It takes some doing as they don't exist').

The poems in this collection roam around, wining and dining themselves from Cork to New York, Tripoli to Sabratha, Berlin to Seville. In this way, *Inquisition Lane* is a kind of picaresque led not necessarily by a character, but by a voice, or a way of seeing. It is a gallivant through a world partly ours and partly not; real places are charmed and refigured by the imagination. Perhaps like the Mallow Races, we can visit these places, but the places of these poems are not to be found there.

Colm Breathnach

THE LISTENERS

An múinteoir matamaitice a dhein,
mar gheall ar bhabhta neamh-aistir éigin,
é a chur de phionós orm
'The Listeners' le Walter de la Mare
a chur do ghlanmheabhair
agus a aithris os comhair an ranga go léir,
chuir sé comaoin orm
nár thuig sé féin, b'fhéidir, ag an am.

Daichead bliain nach mór ó scaramar go deireanach le chéile
deirim an dán arís anois do na compánaigh léinn sin.
'Is there anybody there?', a fhiafraím os ard
agus macallaíonn na focail i measc na scáileanna.

Deirim an dán iomlán arís don rang
agus don Máistir Ó Donnagáin,
'... thronging the faint moonbeams on the dark stair
That goes down to the empty hall'.

Deirim an t-iomlán dóibh siúd a éisteoidh
agus dóibh siúd fiú nach féidir leo.

Agus nuair a thagaim go deireadh an dáin,
nuair a deirim 'When the plunging hoofs were gone',
tuileann an tost ar ais go socair mar is gnách
agus tuileann ar ais arís an neamhshuim iomlán san.

Eleanor Hooker

MISCONDUCT

> *Decoded, the message etches itself in acid*
> *so every syllable becomes a sore.*
> – Ruth Stone (*The Wound*)

An endless after-dinner speech
and I wait for a pause before returning to my seat.
A porcelain doll waits too.
Her rusty-blue eyes fix on me.
She smiles an immaculate sort of malice.
I don't know her, but wonder how she died.
"I know your sister," she says. "I worked with her …
professionally." I name my sisters, but *no* and *no*
and *no*. She grows impatient, snaps her name.
She leans close. I smell starvation on her breath,
hear a mechanism, no-one could call a heart, thud.
"You see," she says "I was her therapist."

A trap – steel crushes my ankles.
I know this race of people, I withdraw into history
to find my sister, take her by the hand and run.

We escape through tall grass in the back meadow,
through a field of dandelion clocks tick-tocking
beside the railway track. Down at the river
we hunker beneath the bridge,
laugh at this bold new adventure.
Too young to own a lexicon for our future,
we speak nursery rhymes half learned –
Needles and pins,
needles and pins.
When a doll comes to life,
your trouble begins!
She says she wants to go home
and I return to myself.

The speeches continue
but I have retreated so far
I hear only faint resounds.
The living doll cannot reach me,

though her silence says, don't get drunk
on any assumption you are accepted here.

And I return to myself.
My sister says she wants to go home.
Your trouble begins
when a doll comes to life.
Needles and pins,
needles and pins.
We speak nursery rhymes half learned –
too young to own a lexicon for our future
we laugh at this bold new adventure.
We hunker beneath the bridge
beside the railway track. Down at the river
we run through a field of dandelion clocks tick-tocking,
to escape through tall grass in the back meadow.

Damian Smyth

THE LEGANANNY DOLMEN

She was understood as something like those stones,
Under and through and into the belly of which
Infants would be passed to be cured of shingles,
Styes, tics, measles – earth ailments in the first instance,
Conflagrations, eruptions, now and in time to come.
On the other side, a cradle of hands was waiting
And a big face, soft and remarkably bearded, smiling,
So that I understood in turn the old tale of Androcles,
The thorn black and rooty as a nail in the paw,
As a simple talisman of fear's proximity to love:
Under the big top, the bucket filled with confetti,
The high wire strung from a platform to the stars,
No net; the clooty tusk drawn softly from the pad.
In her own case, though, when bed-ridden, her hip
Shrunk to a bloody gel in a wound big as a fist,
There was not even a handful of damp moss,
Scraped from the green side of the boulders,
To settle in the hole: but soggy linens, smoke,
The sweet presence of decay under the sheets,
Her bony hand fast, blindly, in silence, in my own.

Notes on Contributors

Graham Allen is Professor of English at University College Cork. He was the winner of the 2010 Listowel Poetry Prize and has been shortlisted for various other awards, including the Listowel First Collection Prize, the Crashaw Poetry Prize, The Fool for Poetry Prize, and the Shine / Strong First Collection Prize. His e-poem 'Holes', and his collections *The One That Got Away* (2014) and *The Madhouse System* (2014), are published by New Binary Press. *Decade One: Holes* 2006-2016 is due for publication this year.

Colm Breathnach: File, úrscéalaí, agus aistritheoir. Seacht gcinn de chnuasaigh filíochta atá foilsithe aige móide rogha dánta agus an leabhar is déanaí uaidh, *Tírdhreacha* (*Leabhair*COMHAR, 2015), ar rogha dánta agus dánta nua atá ann. Tá dánta leis aistrithe go hocht gcinn de theangacha. Poet, novelist, and translator. He has published seven collections of poetry along with a selected edition and his latest, *Tírdhreacha* (*Leabhair*COMHAR, 2015), which contains selected and new poems. He has had poems translated into eight languages.

Michael Brophy lives in Belfast, and has lived and worked on education programmes in Africa, South America, and the Middle East. His poetry has been published in journals and anthologies including *Poetry Ireland Review*, *Hibernia*, *Creative Commotion*, *Rhyme & Reason*, and *Sing Freedom*. His collection, *A Tired Tribe*, was published by Blackstaff Press.

Paddy Bushe is a poet, editor, and translator. He has published ten collections of poetry, eight in English and two in Irish, as well as four books of translations. His most recent collection, *On A Turning Wing* (Dedalus Press, 2016), won the *Irish Times* Poetry Now Award for 2017. He is a member of Aosdána.

Moya Cannon has published five collections of poetry; her most recent, *Keats Lives* (2015), is published by Carcanet Press. She has edited *Poetry Ireland Review*, and was 2011 Heimbold Professor of Irish Studies at Villanova University. Her *Collected Poems* will be published by Carcanet in 2018.

Alvy Carragher's first collection, *Falling in Love with Broken Things*, is published by Salmon Poetry. She was part of the 2016 Poetry Ireland Introductions readings, representing the series at an event in New York. She graduated from the National University of Ireland Galway with a Masters in Writing, and returned to mentor / teach the third-year poetry workshop in 2016 and 2017.

Gerard Coughlan grew up in Grosvenor Place and Evergreen Road, Cork City. An appreciation of nature comes from his late mother, from West Cork; and an eye for detail comes courtesy of his late father, a Master bookbinder. He has published a collection of poetry, *Jigsaw Fields*.

Martina Dalton has a background in visual art, having studied fine art at Waterford Institute of Technology. She began writing poetry through her study of literature and creative writing at Waterford College of Further Education. 'Lilac' in this issue is her first published poem.

Deirdre Daly is a writer living in Dublin. Her poetry has been published in *Magma, Banshee, Crannóg, The Minnesota Review,* and elsewhere. She was nominated for a 2017 Hennessy New Irish Writing award, and was the poetry winner of the 2016 Over the Edge New Writer Competition.

Clodagh Beresford Dunne received the 2016 Arts Council of Ireland Emerging Writer bursary. In the same year, as part of Culture Ireland's international programme, she delivered a series of readings, interviews, and lectures in Pittsburgh. A qualified lawyer and teacher, she lives in Dungarvan, Co Waterford with her husband and four children.

Gerard Fanning's *Hombre: New and Selected Poems* was published in 2011, and in 2013 a further selection was published in *The Wake Forest Series of Irish Poetry, Volume 3* (Wake Forest University Press).

Tomás de Faoite, from Dowth, lives in the Netherlands. His recent poetry has appeared in *Poetry Ireland Review* and *Southword*. Reinart Editions published his first collection, *Dust*, in 1998, while *Green Father* was published by Poëzie-uitgeverij Wel in 2006. He is working on a third collection.

Dominic Fisher is from Bristol. He published in British magazines in the 1980s and 1990s, then disappeared into English language teaching. The poems of his recent return to publishing and performing are often concerned with the relationship between nature and contemporary life.

Patrick FitzSymons, already with an eclectic career behind him, graduated with a M.A. from the Seamus Heaney Centre at Queen's University, Belfast, in 2012. His poetry has been published in Ireland and the UK, and his screenplays have been produced by the BBC and RAI in Italy.

Piotr Florczyk is a poet, essayist, and translator of Polish poetry. His most recent books are *East & West*, a volume of poems, and two volumes of translations: *My People & Other Poems* by Wojciech Bonowicz, and *Building the Barricade* by Anna Świrszczyńska. He lives in Los Angeles.

Kevin Graham's poems have appeared in *The Irish Times*, *The Stinging Fly*, and on RTÉ Radio. Smithereens Press published a chapbook, *Traces*, the title poem of which appeared in *Poetry Ireland Review* 117. He is working on a first collection.

Liam Harrison is a Bristolian writer living in Dublin. He completed an M.Phil. in Irish Writing at Trinity College, Dublin, writing a thesis on Samuel Beckett and Tom Murphy. He is currently developing a digital exhibition with Emeritus Professor Nicholas Grene on the plays of Tom Murphy, for TCD Library.

Seán Hewitt won a Northern Writers' Award in 2016. His poetry has been published in *POETRY*, *The Poetry Review*, and *The New Statesman*, among other outlets. He is currently a Ph.D. candidate at the Institute of Irish Studies, University of Liverpool.

Eleanor Hooker has published two poetry collections with Dedalus Press. Her second, *A Tug of Blue*, was published in October 2016. Earlier this year her poem 'By Longing' was a winner of the UK Poetry Society Members poetry competition. She is Programme Curator for the Dromineer Literary Festival, and is helm on Lough Derg RNLI Lifeboat. See **www.eleanorhooker.com**

Fred Johnston's most recent collection of poems is *Alligator Days* (Revival Press, 2013). He has published collections of poetry, short stories and three novels. In the mid-seventies he was a co-founder of the Irish Writers' Co-operative; in 1986, he founded Galway's Cúirt literature festival. His recent poetry has appeared in *The Spectator* and *The New Statesman*, and in 2016 he was a recipient of a Katherine and Patrick Kavanagh bursary.

Ben Keatinge is a Visiting Research Fellow at the School of English, Trinity College, Dublin. He is currently editing a volume of essays on the poetry of Richard Murphy entitled *Making Integral: Critical Essays on Richard Murphy*, to be published in 2018.

Roisin Kelly was born in Belfast, raised in Leitrim, and currently lives in Cork. Her work has previously appeared in *Poetry*, *The Stinging Fly*, *Lighthouse*, and *Headstuff*. Her chapbook *Rapture* was published in 2016 by Southword Editions. She won the Fish Poetry Prize 2017, and is assistant editor of *The Penny Dreadful*. See **www.roisinkelly.com**

Susan Kelly is from Westport, Co Mayo. Her work has appeared in many journals, including *Cyphers, Crannóg, Revival, Abridged, The London Magazine, Boyne Berries, The Stony Thursday Book*, and *The Ogham Stone*. She was shortlisted for the Writing Spirit Award (2010), the Over the Edge New Writer of the Year (2013), and longlisted for the WOW award in 2014.

Noel King was born and lives in Co Kerry. His poetry collections are published by Salmon Poetry: *Prophesying the Past*, (2010), *The Stern Wave* (2013), and *Sons* (2015). From 2003 to 2013 he edited almost fifty Irish poetry titles for Doghouse Books, and was poetry editor of *Revival Literary Journal* for 2012/13. See **www.noelking.ie**

Aoife Lyall is an Irish poet living in the Scottish Highlands. She was shortlisted for the 2016 Hennessy New Writers Award and the 2017 Jane Martin Prize. Her work has appeared in *The Irish Times, The Stinging Fly, The Poets' Republic*, and *Northwards Now*, among other outlets. She is currently writing her first collection.

Seán Lysaght's first collection, *Noah's Irish Ark*, was published by Dedalus Press in 1989. He has since published six collections of poems and translations, including *Erris* (The Gallery Press, 2003), *The Mouth of a River* (The Gallery Press, 2007), and *Carnival Masks* (The Gallery Press, 2014). A new work in prose, *Eagle Country*, is forthcoming from Little Toller.

Michael McCarthy was born in West Cork and lives in North Yorkshire. He is a former winner of the Patrick Kavanagh Award, and his most recent collection, *The Healing Station*, was described by Anne Enright as 'life at its most challenging made beautiful on the page', and chosen by Hilary Mantel in *The Guardian* Best Books of 2015.

Ben McGuire is a teacher and translator living in Dublin. His poems have appeared in *The Irish Times, Cyphers*, and *Poetry Ireland Review*.

Jennie Malboeuf is a native of Kentucky. Her poems are found in the *Virginia Quarterly Review, Oxford Poetry, The Hollins Critic, AGNI, Epoch, New American Writing, Alaska Quarterly Review, New South, Poetry Northwest*, and *Best New Poets 2016*. She teaches writing at Guilford College in North Carolina.

Mary Montague's poetry collections are *Black Wolf on a White Plain* (Summer Palace Press, 2001) and *Tribe* (Dedalus Press, 2008). She completed a Ph.D. in birdsong in 2014. She has been widely published in journals and anthologies, most recently in *Washing Windows? Irish Women Write Poetry* (Arlen House, 2017).

Julie Morrissy's debut collection *Where, The Mile End* is forthcoming in 2019 with BookThug (Canada). In 2016 her pamphlet *I Am Where* (Eyewear Publishing) was shortlisted for the Saboteur Awards and she was selected as a Poetry Ireland 'Rising Generation' poet. She is currently pursuing her Ph.D. by practice at Ulster University.

John O'Donnell's work has been published and broadcast widely. His awards include the Irish National Poetry Prize, the Ireland Funds Prize, a Hennessy Award for Poetry, and a Hennessy Award for Fiction. He has published three poetry collections. *Nighthawks: New and Selected Poems* is forthcoming in 2018.

Killian O'Donnell's work has been published in *The Moth*, *Poetry Ireland Review*, *New Irish Writing*, *The Stinging Fly*, *THE SHOp*, *Poetry Daily* (USA), and elsewhere. He lives in Co Galway.

Mary O'Donnell is a widely-published poet and fiction writer. Her seventh collection, *Those April Fevers*, was published in 2015 (Arc Publications). She has also written four novels and two collections of short fiction. She currently teaches poetry on the M.A. in Creative Writing at NUI Galway. She is a member of Aosdána. See **www.maryodonnell.com**

Nessa O'Mahony is a Dublin-born poet. She has published four books of poetry – *Bar Talk* (1999), *Trapping a Ghost* (2005), *In Sight of Home* (2009), and *Her Father's Daughter* (2014). She is co-editor with Siobhán Campbell of *Eavan Boland: Inside History* (Arlen House, 2016), and produces the regular literary podcast, *The Attic Sessions*, with her husband Peter Salisbury. She is a Lecturer in Creative Writing with the Open University.

Cathal Ó Searcaigh's latest collections include *An Fear Glas: The Green Man* (Arlen House, 2015), *An Bhé Ghlas* (Leabhar Breac, 2016), and *Out of the Wilderness* (The Onslaught Press, 2016), with translations by Gabriel Rosenstock. Leabhar Breac will publish his novel, *Teach an Gheafta*, later this year. With Chris Agee, he edits *Irish Pages*. He is a member of Aosdána.

Chris Preddle retired from library work to a green valley below the Pennines. His second collection, *Cattle Console Him*, was published by Waywiser in 2010. His third collection, *The May Figures*, will be published by Eyewear Publishing in 2018. His work has appeared in *Irish Pages*, *THE SHOp*, *The Yellow Nib*, and many British magazines.

Caroline Price is a violinist and teacher living in Suffolk. She has published three collections of poetry, with a fourth due from Shoestring Press later this year. She also publishes short stories, and in 2015 was runner-up for the Society of Authors' Tom Gallon award for short fiction.

Prayag Ray was born in India and is currently writing a Ph.D. in English at Queen's University, Belfast. His poems have appeared in *The Honest Ulsterman* and on *The Lifeboat* website. His non-fiction has appeared in *The Tangerine*. He is an editor with *The Open Ear*.

Nell Regan's latest poetry collection is *One Still Thing* (Enitharmon Press, 2014), and her biography, *Helena Molony: A Radical Life 1883-1967*, is just out with Arlen House. She was a 2016 Patrick and Katherine Kavanagh Fellow. See **www.nellregan.com**

Matthew Rice was born in Belfast. Poems have appeared on both sides of the Atlantic, and in the anthology *The Best New British and Irish Poets 2017* (Eyewear Publishing). He was awarded runner-up in the Seamus Heaney Award for New Writing 2017, and was a participant in this year's Poetry Ireland Introductions Series.

Breda Wall Ryan lives in Bray, Co Wicklow. Language, nature and mythology are driving forces in her poetry, which is widely published, translated, and broadcast. Among her many awards are The Gregory O'Donoghue International Poetry Prize, and the iYeats Poetry Prize. In 2016, *In a Hare's Eye* (Doire Press) won the Shine / Strong Award for a first collection.

Stephen Sexton lives in Belfast. His poems have appeared in *Granta*, *Poetry London*, *Poetry Ireland Review*, and *Best British Poetry 2015*. His pamphlet, *Oils*, published by The Emma Press, was a Poetry Book Society's Winter Pamphlet Choice. He was the winner of the 2016 National Poetry Competition, and the recipient of an ACES award from the Arts Council of Northern Ireland.

Danny Sheehy: File, iascaire, fear déanta naomhóg agus taistealaí ab ea Domhnall Mac Síthigh (Danny Sheehy), a bádh go tragóideach sa Spáinn í mí an Mheithimh 2017. Foilsíodh an dán seo cheana in *Súil Seilge*.

Peter Sirr has published ten collections with The Gallery Press, most recently *Sway* (2016), versions of poems from the troubadour tradition. *The Rooms* (2014) was shortlisted for the *Irish Times* Poetry Now Award and the Pigott Poetry Prize. *The Thing Is* (2009) was awarded the Michael Hartnett Prize in 2011.

Fiona B Smith won the poetry section of the 2012 Over the Edge New Writer of the Year competition. She has had poetry published in *Southword, Crannóg, Hennessy New Irish Writing, The Galway Review*, and the Templar Poetry anthology, *Skein*. She translates from Scandinavian languages and reports for the German Press Agency.

Damian Smyth's five collections are *Downpatrick Races* (2000), The *Down Recorder* (2004), *Lamentations* (2010), *Market Street* (2010), and *Mesopotamia* (Templar 2014). *English Street* is due in 2018.

Declan Sweeney has had stories and poems published in *London Magazine, Cyphers, The Stinging Fly, The Moth, Icarus, Revival, Crannóg, Stand,* and elsewhere. He was shortlisted for the Listowel Poetry Collection Prize, and has also written for radio and the stage.

Betty Thompson's poems have appeared in various periodicals, and on the websites of the Irish Film Institute and Coffee House Poetry. Her work is included in the anthology *If Ever You Go: A Map of Dublin in Poetry & Song* (Dedalus Press, 2014). In 2009 Scallta Media published her collection *Painting the Vestibule*.

Alan Titley is a scholar, novelist, playwright and poet. His *An Bhean Feasa* (Cló Iar-Chonnacht, 2014), on the life and times of the Irish servant Goody Glover, who was hanged in Boston in 1688, is the longest poem in modern Irish.

Gráinne Tobin lives in Newcastle, Co Down. Her books are *Banjaxed* (2002) and *The Nervous Flyer's Companion* (2010), both from Summer Palace Press. She has contributed to *Word of Mouth* (Blackstaff Press), *When the Neva Rushes Backwards* (Lagan Press), *On the Grass When I Arrive* (Liberties Press), *Washing Windows? Irish Women Write Poetry* (Arlen House), and *Something About Home* (Geographies Publications).

Jessica Traynor's first collection, *Liffey Swim*, was published by Dedalus Press in 2014 and shortlisted for the Shine / Strong Award. A series of poems commissioned by The Salvage Press, in response to Jonathan Swift's *A Modest Proposal*, is forthcoming later this year. Her awards include the Ireland Chair of Poetry Bursary and the Hennessy New Writer of the Year Award. She reviews poetry and prose for RTÉ's *Arena, Sabotage Reviews*, and *The Sunday Times*.

Eriko Tsugawa-Madden was born in Hokkaido in Northern Japan and moved to Ireland in 1989. She writes poems in both English and Japanese. Her first bilingual poetry book, *Bride of the Wind*, was published in 2013. She lives in Dublin.

Mary Woodward is a Londoner with Welsh and Irish parents (Ceredigion and South Sligo). Her collection – *The White Valentine* (Worple Press) – was highly commended for a Forward Prize in 2014. Her recent work placed in the Gregory O'Donoghue prize in 2016, and is also published in *The Stinging Fly* ('In the Wake of the Rising' issue).

Enda Wyley has published five collections of poetry, most recently *Borrowed Space: New and Selected Poems* (Dedalus Press, 2014). She was the inaugural winner of the Vincent Buckley Poetry Prize, and the recipient of a Patrick and Katherine Kavanagh Fellowship, 2014. She is a member of Aosdána.